THE BEATLES

THE BEATLES

THE
BEATLES

THE BEATLES

BILL YENNE

LONGMEADOW
PRESS

ACKNOWLEDGMENTS

We wish to thank Tom Schultheiss, Harry Castleman and Walter J Podrazik, whose important scholarship and reference works were essential to this book. We'd also like to thank the four Beatles for the music that makes this book still viable more than 20 years after Sgt Pepper taught the band to play. A final word of thanks is due to Gail Rolka for typing the manuscript.

Edited by Tom Debolski and Timothy Jacobs

Designed by Bill Yenne

PHOTO CREDITS
Apple Corps Ltd: 44, 54-55, 57, 60-61 *(all)*, 65-66, 67, 68, 69, 70-71 *(all)*, 72, 73 *(both)*, 74, 75 *(both)*, 77, 78, 79, 83 *(top)*, 84, 85 *(top)*, 86, 87, 90, 91, 92, 92-93. **Atlantic Records**: 51 *(top right)*, 100. **British Tourist Board**: 8-9. **Capitol Records**: 1, 31, 40-41, 43, 49. **Cinema Collectors**: 2-3, 7, 10, 11, 12, 13, 14, 21, 22 *(both)*, 23 *(top)*, 25 *(bottom)*, 28-29, 34-35, 37 *(bottom)*, 38 *(all)*, 42-43, 47, 48, 50 (lower left), 52, 52-53, 62 (left), 64, 80, 88 *(top left)*. **Columbia Records**: 50 *(lower right)*, 88 *(bottom)*. **Melanie Earnshaw**: 6-7. **EMI/Parlophone**: 17, 18, 19, 26, 37, 45, 101. **London Records**: 51 *(left, both)*. **MCA**: 51 *(lower right)*, 85 *(bottom)*. **Odeon**: 27. **RCA**: 50 *(top right)*. **20th-Century Fox**: 96, 97 *(all)*, 98-99. **United Artists Films**: 20, 23 *(bottom)*, 24 *(both)*, 25 *(top)*, 30, 32, 33, 36, 37 *(top)*, 88 *(top right)*, 89. ©**Bill Yenne**: 4-5, 50 *(top left)*, 58-59, 62-63, 82, 83 *(lower right)*, 94, 94-95 *(all)*, 110.

C O N T E N T S

COME TOGETHER

'Well my heart went zoom, when I crossed that room.'
–*John Lennon and Paul McCartney (1962)*

They were, in the words of John Lennon, 'The Greatest Show On Earth.' That says it all. They were the biggest concert draw of their time; they were the most important and popular musical phenomenon in this century. Even the Rolling Stones didn't start calling themselves 'the greatest rock and roll band in the world' until *after* the Beatles broke up. Their records outsold all their competitors during the 1960s. Twenty years after they stopped recording, their recordings still outsell the work of many current bands.

Their music and lyrics changed the lives of a generation–and the generation that followed. Twenty years later, another generation–people too young to ever have had a chance to hear them live–draws both pleasure and inspiration from their music.

The Beatles were simply 'four lads from Liverpool' who came together by chance to form an alchemical reaction that could be seen, heard and felt, yet could not be fully understood. The power of the Beatles was always much greater than the sum of the four parts. It was a magic borne of the *harmony* of those four parts.

Our purpose in this book, however, is not to analyze or attempt to interpret the phenomenon, but rather to tell the story of those 'four lads from Liverpool' and the decade they helped to define.

The story begins in a great port city at the mouth of the river Mersey in the early 1950s. Liverpool, like most of England's industrial north, was in the midst of an epoch of postwar decline and decay. A port city on the skids, it was a tough town, not an easy place to grow up. Yet half a million souls existed there in somber row houses on sooty streets, barely noticing the few sad remnants of once proud Victorian splendor that peeked through the downside of the industrial revolution.

Being a major port, however, Liverpool was on the leading edge of cultural imports from the United States, a society whose mid-1950s vibrance was in stark contrast to the gray mood of Liverpool. Among the artifacts that seeped into the 'Liddypool' youth culture were seven-inch recordings of the new American musical style that was called 'rock and roll.' A mixture of blues and country, its rhythm seemed to have an amazing power over young people that couldn't be understood by anyone born before 1940. Suddenly, Americans like Bill Haley, Carl Perkins and Elvis Presley, who were unknown in the United States six

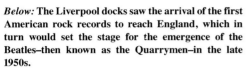 **MERSEY BEAT**

Vol. 1 No. 13   JANUARY 4–18, 1962   Price THREEPENCE

Below: The Liverpool docks saw the arrival of the first American rock records to reach England, which in turn would set the stage for the emergence of the Beatles–then known as the Quarrymen–in the late 1950s.

By 1962 the band had undergone a number of name–as well as personnel–changes, and *Mersey Beat*, the local musicians' paper, proclaimed them Liverpool's top 'skiffle' group in *MB*'s popularity poll.

Right: The front page of the 4 January 1962 *Mersey Beat*, featuring *(from left to right)* John Lennon, George Harrison, Paul 'McArtrey' (the paper misspelled his name) and Pete Best. In the photo, Best appears removed from the group–as he would soon be.

months before, became cult figures around the world. By 1956, it seemed that every teenager in Liverpool who could afford a guitar was a member of a 'skiffle group,' as Liverpool rock bands were then known.

John Winston Lennon was the first of the men who eventually became the Beatles to form a skiffle group. Born 9 October 1940 during a German air raid on Liverpool, Lennon's middle name was borrowed from the wartime Prime Minister. He spent his first five years with his mother Julia in Liverpool's Penny Lane district after his father, Alfred, a merchant seaman, ran away to sea. In 1945, after World War II ended, Alfred Lennon returned briefly, planning to take John to New Zealand, but ultimately sailed away alone, gone from his young son's life forever.* Julia, who felt unable to cope with John, farmed the young lad out to her sister Mimi and brother-in-law George Smith.

Mimi and George Smith lived in suburban Mendips near a rambling estate named, coincidentally, 'Strawberry Fields.' This estate, with its extensive grounds, was to become a favorite playground for young John. Despite rejection by both of his natural parents, John Lennon grew up in relatively more comfortable surroundings than most of the people who were members of his early skiffle groups. He formed his first such band–the Quarrymen–in 1956 when he was 15 years old and a student at Liverpool's Quarry Bank High School.

The Quarrymen played for school functions and other small gatherings, and it was at one such affair–a picnic in suburban Wooton on 15 June 1956–that Lennon was introduced to another guitar player named James Paul McCartney, whom he invited to join the band.

James Paul McCartney, who went by the name 'Paul,' was born 14 years and three days earlier, on 18 June 1942, the son of Jim and Mary McCartney. Mary had died only a few months before Paul's fourteenth birthday and he had spent the intervening time losing himself in his guitar playing. His proficiency made the young left-hander attractive to Lennon, and McCartney quickly became an important part of Lennon's skiffle quartet.

A year later, the Quarrymen made their first semi-professional recording. Percy Phillips, the studio owner, later recorded over the tapes to save a few quid, thus depriving the world of the very first Lennon-McCartney recording session.

It was in 1958 that John and Paul were first introduced to George Harrison. Born 25 February 1943, Harrison had joined his first band, the Rebels, in 1956 at the age of 13, shortly after buying his first guitar. George became a member of the Quarrymen in 1958. The band soon began to perform occasionally under the name Johnny and the Moondogs.

By 1959, the Quarrymen/Moondogs–consisting of Lennon, McCartney and Harrison on guitar, Thomas Moore on drums and Stuart Sutcliffe on bass–became the central focus of the band members' lives. They all quit school to devote full time to the band, which attempted to crack the surly bonds of the big time at talent shows from Liverpool to Manchester. By November, however, economic reality took over and the group disbanded.

Early in 1960, Lennon reassembled the band for another try under a new name. Having decided not to bill the group as either the Quarrymen or the Moondogs, John decided on the name 'Silver Beatles,' a pun on the words 'beat' and 'beetle,' while

Right: Central Liverpool in characteristic grays looking toward the River Mersey. Not shown are the ships which no longer ply these waters for Queen and Empire.

also being a tongue-in-cheek tribute to Buddy Holly's band, the Crickets.

Their first major break came in April 1960, when the Silver Beatles were hired by promoter Larry Parnes as the backup band for Johnny Gentle's Scottish tour. Then, on 6 June, they were booked into Grosvenor Ballroom in Wallasey along with Gerry and the Pacemakers, another Liverpool band which also made it big in the 1960s.

Shortly after this concert, the Silver Beatles decided to travel even farther afield in search of show business fame and fortune, this time traveling to the German port city of Hamburg. Meanwhile, Paul McCartney had invited 19-year-old Liverpool drummer Pete Best to join them for the Hamburg adventure.

Leaving Liverpool on 16 August, they played their first club date the next night, filling in for Cass and the Casanovas at the Indra Club. After this initial success, they were booked on 18 August for a two-month run at the club. When the Indra Club was shut down by Hamburg Police in October, the Silver Beatles went to work at the nearby Kaiserkeller, where they performed for another two months, when three of the four were deported. George Harrison, aged 17, was deported for being a year too young to play in bars, while Paul and Pete were deported for having started a fire in the squalid room they were sleeping in at the Indra. John Lennon, finding himself alone in Germany, gathered up as much of their equipment as he could, and made his way back to England.

At that same time, there was another Liverpool band–Rory Storm and the Hurricanes–also playing at the Kaiserkeller. Occasionally, when Pete Best was absent, the Hurricane drummer, Richard Starkey (aka Ringo Starr), would sit in with the Beatles. A demo record was made during this time on which Lennon, McCartney and Harrison of the Beatles joined Lu

Walters and Ringo Starr for *Fever*, *September Song* and *Summertime*.

By the time the Beatles returned to Liverpool (just before Christmas), the rock scene at home had mushroomed. There were hundreds of bands playing at dozens of clubs. Among these clubs were the Casbah and the Cavern, where the Beatles began playing occasional dates in early 1961, between concert appearances in such venues as the Grosvenor Ballroom in Wallasey and the Hambleton Hall in Liverpool.

Despite achieving some measure of success at home, the Beatles were still anxious to get back to the wild, bawdy scene that prevailed in Hamburg. John Lennon applied for his second German visa on 28 February 1961, although the Beatles didn't arrive on Hamburg's notorious 'Reeperbahn' until April. Once there, the group was booked for a three month engagement at the Top Ten Club, the same club where they had played one date the previous December.

In May 1961, they met Tony Sheridan, a British expatriate band leader then based at the Star Club in Hamburg, and he invited them to be his backup band for a recording session. They did this backup for him under the pseudonym 'Beat Brothers,' and used the same obscure name to record some songs on which Lennon and McCartney sang the lead. In June, when the Beatles were returning to Liverpool, Polydor Records released the first single from the recording session: *My Bonnie (Lies Over the Ocean)* b/w *The Saints (Go Marchin' In)*. In the mid-60s, after the Beatles became famous, Polydor released dozens of different compilations of the songs from these sessions to capitalize on their huge success. It was in June of 1961 that the bearded, introspective Stu Sutcliffe decided to leave the group and stay on in Germany to marry his German girlfriend, artist Astrid Kirschner.

An icon for the Beatles–as well as sensational advertising for Hugo Haas and his freight car company–is this 1961 photo of the band as it existed in the early Hamburg days. *Above, from left to right:* Pete Best, George Harrison, John Lennon,

Paul McCartney and the mysterious Stu Sutcliffe who remained in Hamburg when the rest went back to London. *Facing page:* Lead guitarist George Harrison on a Liverpool street corner, when he was 'just seventeen.'

Back in Liverpool, the Beatles, now a quartet with Lennon and Harrison on guitar, McCartney on bass and Best on drums, found themselves regarded as one of the hottest groups in town. After a 'welcome home' night at the Cavern on 14 July, the group became a regular feature at the club, and by September a 'Beatles fan club' had been formed. By October 1961, copies of the single *My Bonnie* that Polydor had released in Germany in June were cropping up on the Liverpool grey market, although it was still not officially sold in Britain.

On 29 October, a boy named Raymond Jones went into a Liverpool record shop to ask for a copy of *My Bonnie*. The manager of the store was one Brian Epstein, whose family owned a chain of such shops, called North England Music Stores (NEMS). Epstein told the boy that he didn't have it and, upon checking, discovered that it was simply not commercially available north of the Channel. Epstein, who had heard of the Beatles and their impact on the local scene, was very intrigued by what he saw as an emerging regional phenomenon.

Here was a young (only Lennon was over 21) group that was increasingly popular in Liverpool and who had made a big enough name for themselves in Germany that they had already been invited to make a record. Epstein attended their show at the Cavern Club on 9 November, and a month later, on 3 December,

invited them into his office to discuss becoming their manager. Ten days later a contract was formally signed.

History had been made. Though Epstein's efforts initially led to nightclub bookings that netted only £12 a night, within three years the scruffy youngsters from the Cavern Club would be transformed–through Epstein's managerial efforts–into the biggest draw in the show business world!

Brian Epstein lost little time in promoting his new clients with avid enthusiasm. It was a role he was born into and one that would consume the rest of his life. Despite his pressing concerns as a record retailer in the middle of the Christmas season, he managed to arrange an audition session with Mike Smith, the 'artist and repertoire' (A&R) director at Decca, one of Britain's largest record companies. The audition took place on New Year's Day, 1962 in Decca's Hampstead studio in London. The 15 songs showcased the Beatles in excellent form. Though never 'officially' released, tapes of the session have circulated for many years among collectors, who find the quality of the performances to be easily on par with the ones the Beatles released commercially the following year.

Just four days after the Decca audition, Polydor released *My Bonnie* in Britain, but its modest success did little to persuade Decca to sign the Beatles to a recording contract. Six weeks later Dick Rowe of Decca informed Brian Epstein that 'guitar groups' were a passing fad and he didn't want the Beatles on the Decca label. Undaunted, Epstein began making the rounds of other record companies in London with copies of the New Year's Day recordings.

The Beatles, meanwhile, undertook their third sojourn into the Hamburg club scene. They arrived on 11 April 1962, and learned that Stu Sutcliffe had died the day before of a brain hemorrhage, after nearly two years of chronic, violent headaches. Nevertheless, they began a seven week run at the Star Club (Tony Sheridan's old stomping ground) on 13 April. While the Beatles were rocking the Star Club, back in London Brian Epstein was attempting to convince George Martin at EMI Records to give the group an audition.

'So, what's from Liverpool?' Martin asked sarcastically before reluctantly agreeing on 9 May to hear the Beatles. The EMI audition took place in London, on 6 June 1962, as the band made their way home from Hamburg. Initially, Martin remained unconvinced and recommended against EMI signing the Beatles. Epstein then went to work, and convinced EMI distributors to put pressure on the EMI headquarters. By the end of July, the groundswell of support for the Beatles was so great that EMI decided to sign them to their Parlophone record label. In the interim, the band had been playing concert and club dates in the north of England–most of them at the Cavern Club in Liverpool–almost continuously since arriving back home.

It was around this time that Epstein, as well as the other band members, realized that the weakest link musically in the band was drummer Pete Best. On 16 August, in a move which is still considered controversial, Brian Epstein fired Pete Best. The following night at the Cavern, he played his last date as a member of the Beatles, and on 18 August Richard Starkey replaced him as their drummer. Pete Best went on to play with several bands in Liverpool, but within a few years he was out of the music business and working in a bakery.

Richard Starkey, now known universally under the stage name Ringo Starr, was born on 7 July 1940 in Liverpool. When he was

Brian Epstein *(left)* turned North England Music Stores, Ltd–the family business–into an international empire when he 'discovered' the Beatles in 1961. *Facing page:* Harrison, McCartney and Lennon on stage at Liverpool's Cavern Club in 1962, where the Beatles frequently played between their trips to Hamburg.

six years old, he suffered a burst appendix and was forced into a year-long hospital stay that left him a shy and introspective child. Seven years later he developed pleurisy and spent another two years in the hospital. When he was finally released in 1955 at age 15, he had missed so much school that it was considered futile for him to return, so he dropped out to work as a railroad messenger. He received his first set of drums for Christmas when he was 18 and shortly thereafter was asked to join Rory Storm and the Hurricanes.

In the autumn of 1960, Storm and his band played a booking at the Kaiserkeller Club in Hamburg. As we have said previously, it was here that Ringo met, and played music with, John, Paul and George for the first time. The two bands went their separate ways after this, and, although they were active in generally the same musical circles and played the same club circuit in Hamburg and Liverpool, Ringo had little further contact with the Beatles until he was asked to join them in the summer of 1962.

Ringo played his first date with the Beatles on 18 August, and on 3 September both the Hurricanes and the Beatles were together on the bill at Queen's Hall in Widnes. Pete Best, meanwhile, had joined Lee Curtis and The All Stars and was playing concert dates again, but his career had already seen its apogee.

In early September, the Beatles arrived in London for what would be the first of many recording sessions at EMI's studios. The climax of the initial week-long effort came on 11 September 1962, when they recorded the two John Lennon-Paul McCartney songs that would back one another on their first Parlophone single: *Love Me Do* and *PS I Love You*. This record was released less than one month later, on 5 October, and debuted on Radio Luxembourg the same day.

The band continued to appear on stage throughout the north of England during October, and made their first appearance on BBC radio on 26 October, before returning to Hamburg for two weeks at the Star Club.

Their second EMI session came on 26 November, during which they recorded *Please, Please Me*, a song written by Lennon and McCartney a year earlier in Hamburg. Originally, a Mitch Murray song called *How Do You Do It?* was recorded for the A-side at George Martin's insistence, but John hated it and protested. He pushed for *Please Please Me*, and eventually won out. *How Do You Do It?* is found only on bootlegs.

This would become their second single on Parlophone. On 18 December, as *Love Me Do* inched up the charts (it reached 17 on the *Billboard* magazine chart in Britain), the Beatles left for their fifth and last series of club dates on Hamburg's sordid 'Reeperbahn.'

It was during this period that Ted 'King Size' Taylor, another musician from Liverpool, recorded two hours of the Beatles at the Star Club. These tapes were reportedly offered to Brian Epstein for $50, but he rejected them as 'uncommercial.' A decade later, after the Beatles had broken up, the recordings were released as a two-record set in Europe, and were also widely available in the United States. The songs included such rock standards as *Roll Over Beethoven* and *Sweet Little Sixteen*, as well as the first sounding of Lennon and McCartney's *I Saw Her Standing There*. Epstein's opinion to the contrary, most Beatles fans would agree that the recordings represent one of the best (if not *the* best) Beatles concert material ever released.

The magic had been found. The sum of four talents had come together and critical mass had been achieved.

Right: The Beatles on the street in 'Liddypool' in 1962 shortly after Ringo Starr (photo far right) replaced Pete Best as drummer and joined the group on 18 August.

1 9 6 3

I'LL FOLLOW THE SUN

'I feel happy inside, its such a feeling that
my love, I can't hide...You got that something, I think you'll understand...'
–*John Lennon and Paul McCartney (1963)*

The Beatles' world had changed dramatically in 12 months. The first of January 1962 had found them a little-known club band in a recording session that had resulted in disappointment. A year later, the first of January 1963 found them with a much wider following, a recording contract with Britain's largest record company, their first single on the charts and a second single ready for release. They began a brief tour of Scotland on New Year's Day, and *Please Please Me* was released 12 days later. This second single received much more media attention than *Love Me Do* had just three months earlier. By February, after they were given an invitation to appear live on BBC, *Please Please Me* was pushed up to the number two spot on *Billboard* magazine's British Top 20.

The Beatles quickly moved to expand their national exposure in Britain with a pair of back-to-back nationwide tours. Between 2 February and 3 March, they played Liverpool and 18 other cities as part of a tour with pop singer Helen Shapiro, and between 9 March and 31 March they played 21 additional cities as the opening act for the American rockers Chris Montez and Tommy Roe. In the midst of the Helen Shapiro tour, they somehow found time–on 11 February–to go into EMI's Abbey Road studio to record such songs as *I Saw Her Standing There* (working title: *Seventeen*), *Twist and Shout*, *A Taste of Honey*, and another version of *Please Please Me*, that would form the basis for their first Parlophone LP (also called *Please Please Me*), which was released on 22 March. A number of songs from this session, however, such as *I'll Keep You Satisfied*, *Hold Me Tight* and *Keep Your Hands Off My Baby* would still remain unreleased a quarter century later.

On 18 May the Beatles officially began their first British *tour* as headliners, although they had appeared with top billing at five major concerts between 21 April and 15 May, including a 9 May appearance at London's Royal Albert Hall. This tour, which spanned the entire country (including Liverpool), covered 24 cities in 22 days and was followed by an exhausting series of one-night stands. For the Beatles, it was like playing the Cavern Club every night, except that they also had to pack, catch a train, travel 50 or so miles to their next gig, and then unpack nearly a ton of Vox amplifiers and other equipment. However, they were young and bursting with creative energy. Paul would not turn 21 until the end of June, and George was younger still.

By mid-1963 the Beatles had achieved nationwide stardom in England, with a growing legion of devoted fans and fan clubs throughout the country. The foursome suddenly found themselves public personalities, rather than individuals striving for recognition. Even the hair style that the Beatles had adopted (reportedly designed by Stuart Sutcliffe's wife, Astrid) became popular. Almost overnight, schoolboys throughout England were appearing in 'Beatle haircuts'–much to the disgruntlement of their elders.

Large concerts, such as a second performance at Royal Albert Hall on 15 September, replaced club dates, as the smaller sites simply *could not contain* the hordes of adoring fans that streamed in to see the group. Their last performance at Liverpool's Cavern Club was on 3 August 1963, ending a series of what is estimated at more than 300 appearances there in a three-year span.

The Beatles became the hottest thing on the pop music scene in England. *Love Me Do* had struggled and languished in the middle of the charts at the end of 1962, but their third single, *From Me to You*, reached number one only three weeks after it was released on 12 April, and the *Please Please Me* LP had reached the top of the album chart in just two weeks, then held the top slot for six months. The single *She Loves You (Yeah,*

Below and right: Suddenly 1963 was the year of 'the Beatle haircut.' What appears ordinary today was wildly avant garde in 1963. By the end of the year, the group had achieved superstar status throughout England.

Yeah, Yeah) was released on 23 August and promptly hit number one.

Not only were records and concert dates hot items, but other groups began recording, or 'covering,' songs written by John Lennon and Paul McCartney. Billy J Kramer and the Dakotas recorded five of their songs in rapid succession (including *Do You Want to Know a Secret*, which rose to number one), but this was only one of a half dozen groups–including the Rolling Stones–who recorded Lennon-McCartney songs during 1963.

What little was left of their private lives came under intense public scrutiny. A rumor was circulated that John Lennon was actually married to Cynthia Powell, a girl whom he had known since his days at the Liverpool College of Art six years before. They had, in fact, married on 23 August 1962, but this had remained a closely guarded secret for nearly a year despite the birth of their only son, John Charles Julian Lennon, on 8 April 1963.

If there is a specific moment in time when John, Paul, George and Ringo actually stepped across the line from being four guys in a very popular band to being a single entity endowed with almost surreal or supernatural powers, it can probably be pegged to 31 October 1963. On that date, the band flew into London after a five-concert tour of Sweden and were enthusiastically mobbed by thousands of screaming fans. No one was more stunned by this awesome spectacle–which the press dubbed 'Beatlemania'–than the Beatles themselves. After that,

Below: **By late 1963, the Beatles, clad in collarless 'Beatles jackets,' became the object of 'Beatlemania' and were mobbed wherever they went by hordes of Beatlemaniacs** *(at right)* **in rapture over the sight of their idols.** *Facing page:* **The record cover for** *Please Please Me*–**the Beatles' first album.**

screaming throngs became a permanent, ever-present part of their public lives for the next three years.

A six-week concert tour of England and Ireland that began the following day served only underscore the fact that the Beatles had, indeed, become much more than just another rock-and-roll band. Wherever they went on their tour of three dozen cities, the hysteria of their adoring fans seemed only to increase. The screaming fans became so loud that, at times, their music was barely audible. For many, a Beatles concert ceased to be *just* a concert, and became a hysterical experience. Beatlemaniacs overwhelmed police barricades in nearly every city they visited. In Plymouth, fire hoses had to be used to control the crowds.

John Lennon, certainly the most cocky of the four, used the group's newfound popularity to publicly exhibit what was then considered to be almost unheard-of irreverence for the English establishment. At a command performance attended by the

Queen Mother, Princess Margaret and Lord Snowden at London's Prince of Wales Theatre on 4 November 1963, Lennon suggested that the people in the 'cheaper seats' could clap, but those down front could 'just rattle their jewelry.' The Queen Mother was reportedly amused.

By the autumn of 1963, in contrast to one year before, Beatle records were selling incredibly well. On 18 November the group received a 'silver record' for sales of 250,000 copies of the *Please, Please Me* album, and only *four* days later over 300,000 advance copies were announced for their second Parlophone ablum, *With The Beatles*. When finally released, the album first appeared on the *Melody Maker* LP chart a week later–at number one! The single, *I Want to Hold Your Hand*, was released on 29 November with advance orders for 700,000, giving the Beatles seven songs among the Top Twenty hits in Britain.

Under a new contract in America with Capitol Records, *I Want to Hold Your Hand* was released on the day after Christmas in the United States. This was the first release by the company that would control all future American releases of Beatles records and, eventually, tapes and compact discs as well. Prior to this, the only American releases had been the VeeJay album featuring most of the songs from the *Please Please Me* album, and a release of *My Bonnie* on the American Decca label (related to the German Polydor rather than the British Decca).

The marketing clout of a huge organization like Capitol Records insured that Beatle records would be available in stores throughout the United States immediately, that they would be put on the desk of every disc jockey in the country, and that extensive advertising would make the Beatles a household name. The only question remaining as 1963 slipped away and 1964 dawned brightly, was whether American rock-and-roll record buyers would be bitten by the Beatlemania bug.

1 9 6 4

A HARD DAY'S NIGHT

'It's been a hard day's night, and I've been working like a dog. It's been a hard day's night and I should be sleeping like a log.'
–*John Lennon and Paul McCartney (1964)*

The Beatles began 1963 as a modestly successful musical group and ended the year as show business legends. Even the *Times* of London named John Lennon and Paul McCartney as composers of the year, calling their songs 'distinctly ingenious.' *Sunday Times* critic Richard Buckle went a step further and called them the 'greatest composers since Beethoven.'

Even with a new contract with Capitol Records and an American tour under discussion, the reaction of American fans to the Beatles was still an unknown quantity. However, after a slow start in the post-Christmas slump, sales of *I Want to Hold Your Hand* picked up, and by 15 January, it was the number one selling single in the States, with 500,000 copies sold in a 10 day period! The Beatles heard the news while they were in Paris for concerts at the Cyrano and the Olympia. Celebrating at the exclusive George V Hotel, they could look forward to their upcoming American tour without apprehension.

Their trip to the United States began to take shape toward the end of 1963, when New York promoter Sid Berstein booked them for one night in February 1964 at Carnegie Hall. With the sudden popularity of the Beatles in America, Brian Epstein arranged other dates in several cities, and what began as a one-night stand became a full-blown tour. By February, Beatlemania became so rampant in New York that Berstein briefly considered moving the concert from Carnegie Hall to Madison Square Garden.

The arrival of the Beatles at New York's Kennedy Airport on 7 February 1964 was a repeat of their 31 October 1963 entrance into London, but on an even larger scale. Several hundred thousand people jammed the airport to watch the Boeing 707-320 of Pan American Flight 101 carrying the Beatles, as it taxied to the terminal gate. A fleet of Cadillac limousines, sent by Sid Berstein, whisked the foursome off to the Plaza Hotel in

Beatlemania spreads throughout the world–the Beatles on the *Ed Sullivan Show (facing page above)* **in February 1964 and on tour in Paris *(facing page below)* in January 1964.** *Above:* **The Beatles during the filming of *A Hard Day's Night.***

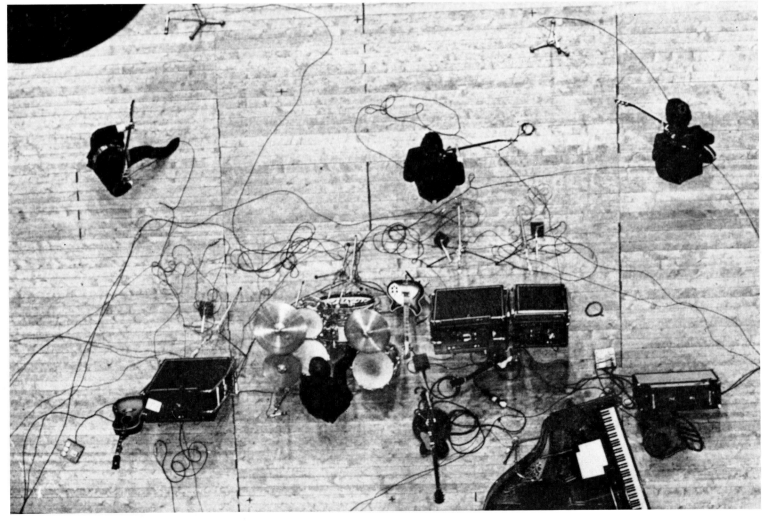

midtown Manhattan. Fans quickly surrounded the hotel, besieging it for a week.

On 9 February, the Beatles performed their first concert in the United States at CBS Television's 53rd Street studio. The concert was broadcast live nationwide on the *Ed Sullivan Show*, attracting the largest one-night audience in the history of television up to that time. Brian Epstein agreed to do the Sullivan Show, even though they were being paid only $2400, because he knew the exposure would prove to be priceless. He was right. Another *Ed Sullivan Show* appearance, taped the same afternoon, would be broadcast two weeks later, on 23 February. On 22 February they went south to play Washington, DC, and on 12 February they returned to New York for two 35-minute shows at Carnegie Hall.

The next day, as press headlines described the Beatles tour as a 'British Invasion,' the group flew to Miami, where they met with a welcome rivaled only by that at Kennedy six days before. On 16 February their fifth American concert was broadcast from Miami live on the *Ed Sullivan Show*.

The Beatles 'conquest' of America in February 1964 is still remembered as a major turning point in the history of rock-and-roll. Suddenly, promoters and record executives were hungry for sounds that would have been dismissed as a novelty only a few months before. Thanks to the Beatles, there was now a vast window of opportunity for the countless hundreds–and eventually thousands–of rock bands that would follow. Once the Beatles touched off the 'British Invasion' of the United States, promoters, unable to book the Fab Four themselves, used any other British band they could find, such as imitators Gerry and

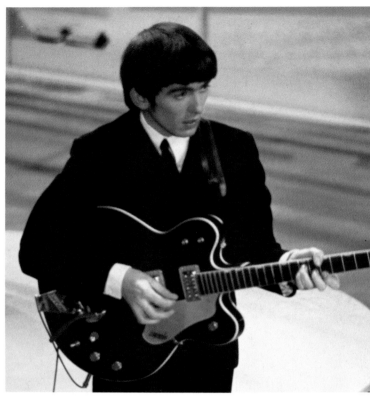

Above: George Harrison on the Ed Sullivan Show in February 1964. *Below:* The Beatles' arrival in New York on 7 February 1964. Thousands of screaming fans rushed to Kennedy Airport to meet them.

the Pacemakers (also from Liverpool and also managed by Brian Epstein). Once the door to the United States market had been opened by the Beatles, countless other British bands–like the Kinks, The Who and the Rolling Stones–who would ultimately play important parts in the evolution of 1960s rock-and-roll, gained access to the American market.

The 1960s rock scene can be said to have actually *begun* on the cold winter day in February 1964 when Bob Dylan first met the Beatles in their room at the Plaza Hotel. The messianic poet laureate of the American folk/beat era met with the reigning deities of rock-and-roll: it was a summit conference of the creative minds that would change the perceptions of an entire generation and would help to define the very culture of the 1960s. After that day, nothing would ever be the same again.

On 2 March 1964, after their triumphant return to London, the Beatles began work on their first feature film, with Richard Lester directing. Ironically dubbed *A Hard Day's Night*, the project had been conceived a few months earlier by British film producer Walter Shenson, as a vignette of 36 hours of the Beatles' lives on the road that would be almost like a documentary. The film begins with a scene filmed on 12 April, of the Beatles running to catch a train at London's Marylebone station while being pursued by hoards of screaming fans, and climaxes with a concert that was filmed at London's Scala Theatre on 26 March.

While *A Hard Day's Night* was in production at Twickenham Studios, Parlophone and Capitol released a half dozen singles in Britain and the United States. In the United States, the new

Above: **The Beatles on the** *Ed Sullivan Show* **in February 1964.** *Below, left to right:* **Director Richard Lester with George Harrison, Ringo Starr and John Lennon on the set of** *A Hard Day's Night* **in March 1964 in London.**

releases went on the charts immediately, giving the Beatles five hits on the American Top 10 and eight in the top 50. On 10 April Capitol released *The Beatles' Second Album*, which was actually *Capitol's* second Beatle album and the *sixth* for the group (counting the Tony Sheridan session, which now had been released in a number of forms). This second Capitol compendium featured mainly recent singles and songs from previous Parlophone albums not included on Capitol's *Meet the Beatles*. Nevertheless, *The Beatles' Second Album* rapidly disappeared off record store shelves and reached the number one slot on American LP charts by early May.

Meanwhile, in Germany, the Odeon label had released a single on 5 March that was composed of the German language versions of *I Want to Hold Your Hand* (*Komm Gib Mir Deine Hand*) and *She Loves You* (*Sie Liebt Dich*), which had been recorded by the Beatles at the Pathe Marconi studio in Paris on 29 January 1964. Aside from the French chorus on *Michelle* (1965), this would be the only foreign language recording ever released by the Beatles. At the same time, Polydor released practically everything from the 1961 'Beatles and Tony Sheridan' sessions, in the single record format to capitalize on the group's immense popularity in Europe.

On 23 March 1964 John Lennon's book–a collection of humorous poems and essays entitled *In His Own Write*–was published in Britain, winning the prestigious Foyle's Literary Prize the same day! Simon & Schuster arranged for the American rights and published it in the United States one month later.

Having conquered Great Britain with their first major tour in December 1963, and the United States with what amounted to a phenomenal four-night stand in February 1964, the Beatles set out on 4 June 1964 to conquer the rest of the world. It was an inauspicious start for Ringo, who collapsed the night before with a 103 degree fever, and subsequently missed the first week

Ringo Starr *(above)* **reading** *Anatomy of a Murder* **on the set of** *A Hard Day's Night*. *Below:* **The Beatles at Scala Theatre in London on 26 March 1964 filming the finale for** *A Hard Day's Night*.

of the tour. With drummer Jimmy Nicol substituting for Ringo, the Beatles played Copenhagen's Tivoli Gardens on 4 June, and then flew south for three shows in suburban Amsterdam on 5 and 6 June, before returning to London to catch a flight to Hong Kong, for two more shows on 10 June.

John, Paul and George, together with Jimmy Nicol, arrived in Adelaide, Australia on 12 June and were met by a throng of 300,000 people–which was later estimated to have been the largest crowd ever to meet them. Ringo, who arrived in Australia the same day, had recuperated and was able to rejoin the group on 16 June for the second of two concerts in Melbourne. After playing Sydney for two shows on 18 and 20 June, they went on to six concerts–two each in New Zealand's three largest cities–before returning to Brisbane, Australia for an appearance on 29 June.

Once back in London, the Beatles, along with Princess Margaret and Lord Snowden, attended the world premier of their movie, *A Hard Day's Night*, on 6 July 1964. They then flew north to its opening in Liverpool four nights later. Within the month the title song, as well as the soundtrack album, had reached number one on the charts in both Britain and the United States. *A Hard Day's Night*–compared by many critics who've seen it to the best of the Marx Brothers films–was put in general release throughout England on 2 August. It opened simultaneously in 500 theaters across the United States on 12 August, after a New York premier the night before.

After a few isolated concert dates in England, two shows in Stockholm (on 23 and 29 July) and very little rest in between, the Beatles embarked on a major North American tour just seven weeks later. Opening on 19 August in San Francisco, they went on to play Las Vegas, Seattle and Vancouver in three nights before arriving in Los Angeles on 23 August for a concert at the Hollywood Bowl–which was recorded by Capitol for a live

Above: **George Harrison relaxing during the filming of** *A Hard Day's Night*. *Below*: **The Beatles with Brian Epstein and Princess Margaret at the world premier of** *A Hard Day's Night* **on 6 July 1964.**

album. The album's release, however, was delayed for a dozen years. The concert itself sold out so fast that even Frank Sinatra and Dean Martin tried, but failed, to get tickets.

The Beatles moved east after Hollywood, playing in another 16 American cities (including two dates in New York), as well as Canada's Montreal and Toronto, before returning to England on 21 September. The hysteria of Beatlemania was in evidence at every stop on this, the first of three annual continent-wide North American tours. Beatlemania was such that, in Cleveland, for instance, a police inspector ordered the group off-stage for five minutes at one point so he could attempt to calm the audience!

Two Beatles albums were released in the United States just before this tour. The *A Hard Day's Night* soundtrack was released on Parlophone in England, and in America, United Artists received the album rights because their film division was handling the release of the movie. The Parlophone version included several current Beatles songs that were not actually on the soundtrack–but United Artists couldn't transgress on Capitol's exclusive contractual domain, so the their version of the *A Hard Day's Night* album had to stay within the bounds of the film's actual materials, and was padded with some George Martin-arranged orchestral versions of Lennon-McCartney songs that *had in fact* been used in the movie soundtrack. Capitol, meanwhile, rushed their third Beatles album into release. Called *Something New*, it actually was a compilation of recent singles, non-movie selections that had appeared on the Parlophone *A Hard Day's Night* album, and three songs from the movie soundtrack that Capitol had previously obtained the rights to release. Those three songs, *I'll Cry Instead*, *If I Fell*, and *I'm Happy Just to Dance With You*, appeared on *both* of the albums in the United States.

The summer of 1964 was marked by a veritable blizzard of

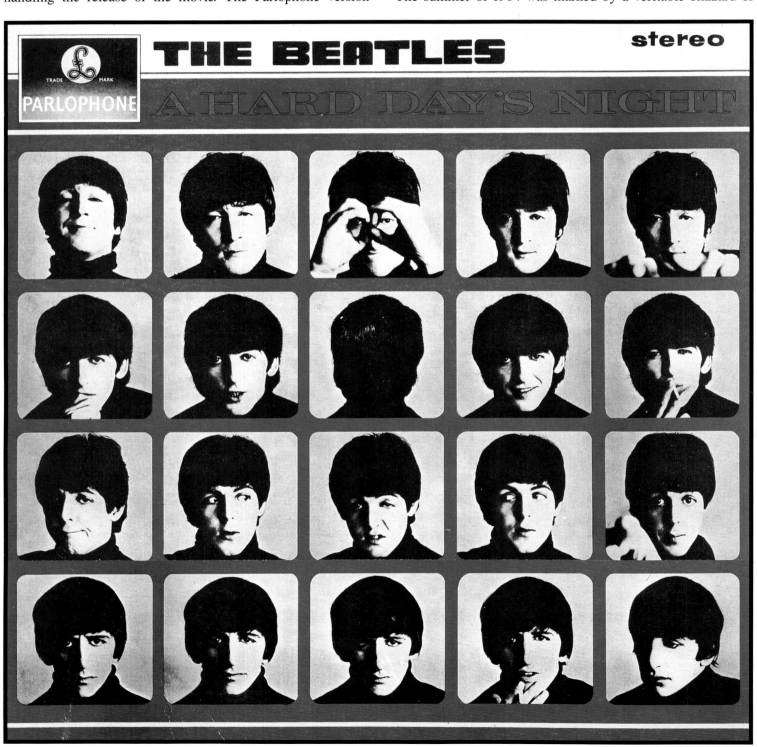

Beatles products. From May through September–in addition to the Capitol, Parlophone and United Artists albums–there were four singles from Capitol, one from Parlophone, an extended play record (four songs) from both companies, and nearly a dozen singles and albums from Polydor and its affiliates, who were still re-releasing the 1961 Tony Sheridan sessions. This was not to mention dozens of releases by Beatles imitators. At the same time, Brian Epstein's NEMS had licensed over 200 firms to manufacture and sell various Beatles souvenirs, which ranged from wigs to bubble gum cards… and from the sublime to the ridiculous.

On 9 October (John Lennon's birthday)–only a week after coming home from the North American tour–the group opened at Bradford on their second annual autumn tour of Britain, which concluded at Bristol a month later.

The fourth Parlophone album, *Beatles for Sale*, was released on 4 December, and two weeks later EMI announced that sales had already topped 700,000. The fourth Capitol album, *Beatles '65*, was released in the United States on 15 December 1964. With a couple of exceptions, it was an abridged version of *Beatles For Sale*, which was in keeping with Capitol's practice of putting 10 or 11 songs on an album, compared to 13 or 14 on most Parlophone albums.

Supported by major tours in both the United Kingdom and North America, as well as the worldwide release of *A Hard Day's Night*, Beatle records sold in vast numbers that exceeded even the most wildly optimistic estimates. In retrospect, it can be said that the all-out hysteria of Beatlemania may have reached its peak in 1964, but still the end was not in sight.

Parlophone's jacket for *A Hard Day's Night* (far left) featured a cinematic collage. This moody Robert Freeman photo for the Parlophone jacket of *Beatles for Sale* (below) was also used by Odeon in Germany.

EIGHT DAYS A WEEK

'When I was younger, so much younger than today, I never needed anybody's help in any way, but now these days are gone I'm not so self assured, now I find I've changed my mind, I've opened up the door.'
–*John Lennon and Paul McCartney (1965)*

After the fantastic successes that the Beatles enjoyed in 1964, they and their manager, Brian Epstein, decided that 1965 would be scheduled using 1964 as a template. The foursome would film a movie in the spring for summer release, tour North America immediately afterward, and then return to Britain for their third annual autumn tour of the United Kingdom.

Parlophone decided to release fewer albums during 1965, projecting that even *if* demand for the Beatles waned during the year, individual records would do as well as they had in 1964 if there were fewer of them. Capitol, however, released four, although the first of these–*The Early Beatles,* released on 22 March–was actually just a repackaging of the old 1963 VeeJay album, which Capitol had bought in order to have all of the Beatles EMI songs under its own umbrella in the United States.

On 22 February the Beatles left London and traveled to the Bahamas to begin work on their second feature-length film. The film was given the working title *Eight Arms to Hold You,* a triple entendre pun that referred variously to the eight arms of the four Beatles; the eight arms of the Hindu deity Kali (a statue of her figured in the film); *and* the eight legs of the long-haired tarantula whose poisonous bite results in frenzied and spasmodic movements embodied in the ritualistic Italian dance 'Tarantella.'

When the single *Ticket to Ride* was released in April, it carried a footnote that indicated that it would appear in the film *Eight Arms to Hold You,* but this is one of only a few artifacts by which the original working title is remembered. In June this title was dropped, and the film was given the title of a song John Lennon

Left: A young John Lennon, songwriter and poet, in 1965. By this time, Lennon had published two collections of prose and poetry—*In His Own Write* and *A Spaniard in the Works*. To some, Lennon was the most creative—and eccentric—Beatle.

I'm a moldy moldy man
I'm moldy thru and thru
I'm a moldy moldy man
You would not think it true.
I'm moldy till my eyeballs
I'm moldy til my toe
I will not dance I shyballs
I'm such a humble Joe.
    –John Lennon

In the introduction to *In His Own Write*, Paul McCartney commented 'There are bound to be thickheads who will wonder why some of it doesn't make sense, and others who will search for hidden meanings.... None of it has to make sense and if it seems funny then that's enough.'

and Paul McCartney had written on 4 April during filming: *Help!*

The Beatles' second film was like *A Hard Day's Night* only insofar as the four group members starred as themselves, and that the plot was a whimsical comedy once again directed by Richard Lester. Beyond this, nearly everything else was different. *Help!* was filmed in color rather than black and white, and its plot was far-fetched and outlandish, whereas the first film played almost like a documentary. The story involved Ringo's acquisition of an outrageous ring, which happened to be the sacred ring of a bizarre and bloodthirsty cult bent on human sacrifice. When Ringo is unable to remove the ring from his finger, an around-the-world chase ensues. In addition to introducing a raft of new Beatles songs, the film showcased a kaleidoscope of cinematic techniques which–seen in retrospect– seem to have presaged, and perhaps even inspired, the rock video style that appeared 20 years later.

Filming on the movie continued in the Bahamas until 12 March, then moved on to the Austrian Tyrol. The Beatles returned to London 10 days later to begin recording the soundtrack for the still untitled film. In early May, after completing

studio scenes at Twickenham Studios, location filming shifted to the Salisbury Plain–where the final shots were filmed near Stonehenge. Production was completed on 12 May, and post-production work was begun.

On 12 June, a week prior to leaving on their European tour, the Beatles were invited to Buckingham Palace, where Queen Elizabeth honored them by naming them as members of the Most Excellent Order of the British Empire. Despite the large amount of revenue that their act had pumped into the country's economy over the preceding 18 months, many former MBE recipients felt insulted that Her Majesty would give such a prestigious award to a rock-and-roll band. These same individuals would probably have been even more outraged had they known that the Beatles had indulged in smoking marijuana in a Palace men's room just prior to their grand audience with the Queen!

The Beatles' European tour, which began on 20 June at the Palais des Sports in Paris and ended at the Barcelona Bullring on

Below: **The Beatles on location in Austria during the third week of March 1965 for the filming of *Help!* The description of the film from the soundtrack album (*facing page*) was enough to make one want to see the film. This was, of course, the idea.**

helicopter to the site of the World's Fair, which was immediately adjacent to Shea Stadium, they made their entrance in an armored car. After all this hoopla, they ran through a dozen songs in a half hour and then quickly departed, $18,000 richer.

Like their previous North American tour, the 1965 tour was comprised of a frenzied succession of one-night stands. This tour, however, was played to generally larger crowds in fewer cities. Only one city in Canada was visited, and stops were scheduled in only three non-coastal cities in the United States. Their visit to Minneapolis turned out to be a mixed blessing. Met at the airport on 21 August by 4000 fans, they earned $2575 a minute during their brief concert. However, in the wee hours of the morning of 22 August, the luster of their wonderful welcome was dulled somewhat when the Minneapolis vice squad intruded on Paul McCartney's hotel room and insisted that the young lady–a fan club president–with whom he was conferring, 'looked sixteen.'

The only break in the hectic tour came between the Beatles' 22 August concert in Portland, and their 29-30 August appearances at the Hollywood Bowl. During this week, the Beatles based themselves at a rented house in Beverly Hills–located at 2850 Benedict Canyon. Here, they entertained a number of people, including members of The Byrds–a southern California group that was soon to make a major splash on the music scene in the United States.

On 27 August they met with Elvis Presley at his secluded home in nearby Bel Air. This is the only known meeting between all four of the Beatles and the 'King of Rock-and-Roll.' Though Presley's career was in abeyance at this point, he was still very highly regarded by musicians and, indeed, all four of the Beatles

considered him to have been the major influence on their early careers back in the late 1950s. John Lennon is recorded as having said that he became a musician *because* of Elvis. In all, this meeting lasted three hours, with all the men playing music and having a good time.

The subject of a joint public appearance, which had been discussed earlier by Brian Epstein and Colonel Tom Parker (Elvis' manager), was not known to have been discussed here. Furthermore, the music that they played together is not known to have been recorded and–because it was a first meeting–likely wasn't. The potential sales of a collection of recorded songs featuring Elvis Presley and all four Beatles would reach into the millions–if, in fact, the session *had been* put on tape. The contractual entanglements between RCA (who handled Elvis' recordings) and EMI/Capitol would, of course, probably deny such a session to fans.

A full range, live, stereo recording of the Beatles was, however, made by Capitol several days later during their concerts at the Hollywood Bowl. These tapes, like those made by Capitol at the Hollywood Bowl a year earlier, were deemed to be commercially unviable because of the background noise of the screaming Beatlemaniacs. As such, the tapes of the 1964 show–and two 1965 shows–languished in Capitol's vaults until 1977, when selections from both were finally released as a single disc album.

A major milestone in Beatles history occurred on 13 September 1965, when Capitol released the song *Yesterday* as a single in the United States. Recorded in June by Paul McCartney alone with an acousitc guitar and included on Parlophone's *Help!* album, *Yesterday* was a slow ballad, unlike other songs the Beatles had

recorded, and very different from anything they'd ever released as a single. It was a milestone for more than that reason. *Yesterday*'s acoustic guitar and string accompaniment gave it a sound that appealed to a wider mass market than the group's earlier music. Also, nearly everything the Beatles had recorded since 1964 was labeled as having been a collaboration between John Lennon and Paul McCartney, but *Yesterday*, although attributed to both, was clearly written and sung by Paul alone. Thus, *Yesterday* can be said to have marked Paul's real debut as a *solo* songwriter.

John and Paul's songwriting partnership originally had begun in the late 1950s, but was not formalized until February 1963– when Northern Songs Ltd was founded to publish their prolific output. This modest venture, which began more as a formality, became a booming business within a year–when the Beatles became popular and the songwriting brilliance of Lennon and McCartney became widely acclaimed. Eventually, both John and Paul began writing individual songs, but because of the legal technicalities associated with Northern, all songs written by either man were credited to the team. Actually, this was *not* inaccurate in most cases because, even if John Lennon arrived at a recording session with a song that was 80 percent complete, Paul McCartney would help to shape the remaining 20 percent. However, *Yesterday* was so evocative of McCartney's compositional style that became almost a theme song for him. John Lennon, too, would later write songs that defined *his* unique style.

For the Beatles, though, *Yesterday* marked a major turning point in their career, because it was able to tap a greater mass audience–and by doing so, it became a 'standard' in popular

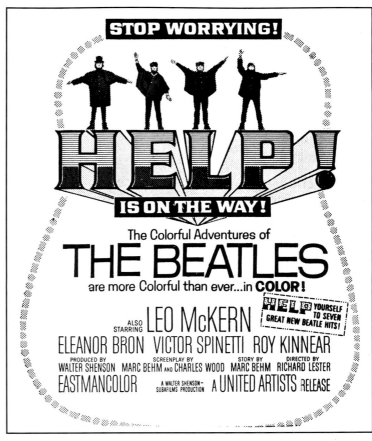

The real and the ideal. The Beatles on stage for the opening scene for *Help!* (*left*) and amid Beatlemaniacs at a real concert (*below*). *Above:* Advertising *Help!*

music. In fact, the sheet music to *Yesterday*–a song that subsequently was recorded by over 500 other artists–ultimately outsold the Beatles single!

The 1965 North American tour marked the end of an era for the Beatles. It was not the end of touring, nor certainly an end to their popularity. Rather, it was the crossroads of a changing musical style that would soon begin to manifest itself in the recording studio. As startlingly wonderful as the early Beatles songs (and the Lennon/McCartney lyrics) had been, they were, for all their popular appeal, simplistic. Seen from today's perspective, the Beatles' early works were just basic rock-and-roll songs.

The world's greatest road show (*below, clockwise from upper left*)–**Paul and George; George alone; and Ringo.** *Opposite:* **Rubber Soul broke new ground and stunned critics when it was released in December 1965.**

In 1965 the landscape of musical style was changing and the Beatles were on the leading edge. As for the lyrics of John Lennon and Paul McCartney, the only figure ahead of them on the horizon was Bob Dylan. His albums *Bringing It All Back Home* and *Highway 61 Revisited* in 1965, and *Blonde on Blonde* in 1966, have a *lyric* complexity that has never been matched. However, in terms of *musical* innovation during the period from 12 October 1965 through the end of the decade, the Beatles *were* the leading edge.

It was on 12 October 1965 that the Beatles stepped into EMI's St John's Wood studio to begin recording the album *Rubber Soul*. This album, like the *Yesterday* single, marked a pivotal point in the evolution of the Beatles' sound. The richness and complexity of the music and lyrics on *Rubber Soul* were so far beyond that of the early *Beatles for Sale* or *Beatles '65*, that today it is hard to believe that these albums were all made in the space of a year.

cover off the jacket to get to the mysterious 'censored' cover beneath. Another recall took place, but not before so many of the records were sold that the album went gold before 8 July.

About this time, another major *faux pas* in the Beatles' career was just beginning to turn into a major controversy. In an interview with Maureen Cleve first published in London's *Evening Standard* on 4 March, John Lennon had stated that the popularity of the Beatles had exceeded that of Christianity. He had intended to say that more people in many Christian countries bought Beatles records and attended Beatles concerts than attended church. Nothing had been further from his mind than to imply that the Beatles were inherently *superior* to Christianity or that they *deserved* to be more popular.

Nevertheless, the phrase 'the Beatles are more popular than Jesus' was taken out of context and quoted in newspapers throughout the world, creating a serious anti-Beatles backlash in many places. The controversy did not, however, prevent their extensive summer tour from being completely sold out. Before the end of the year, Cardinal Cushing, Archbishop of Boston, would concede—albeit reluctantly—that yes, the Beatles were indeed better known throughout the world in 1966 than Jesus.

On 23 June the Beatles left for Germany on the first leg of what was to be their last tour. Billed as a world tour, it actually included stops only in West Germany, Japan and the Philippines, followed by a five-week break, then a two-week North American tour. The first concert was at Circus Krone, in Munich on 24 June. They took a special train to Hamburg the following day, stopping enroute to play a concert at the Grugehalle in Essen. The Hamburg stop marked the first time the Beatles had played in that German port city since December 1962. Aside from Liverpool, the band had played more concerts in Hamburg than in any other city, but the concert on 26 June 1966 would be

the last one.

Having made a brief stopover in Anchorage to avoid a typhoon, the Beatles traveled to Tokyo for a three-night stand at the huge Budokan martial arts stadium on 30 June. This, their only concert appearance ever in Japan, was followed by a single concert in Manila on 4 July. Generally a devoutly Catholic country, the Philippines had been primed by a sensationalist press with John Lennon's controversial statement. This served to whip up the most seriously negative welcome that the Beatles had ever gotten in any city they had played. Having grown accustomed to the enthusiastic greetings they'd received over the years, the Beatles were stunned by the anger and violence in the Philippines and vowed never to return.

The same negativity that manifested itself so pointedly in the Philippines also surfaced in the United States, particularly in the southern states, where there were mass burnings of Beatles *records* and where radio stations made a point of *not* playing Beatles records. Despite John Lennon's public apology in Chicago on 12 August—at the start of the North American leg of their summer tour—several of the Beatles concerts were picketed by various groups such as the Ku Klux Klan, who sent six vocal Klansmen to protest at the show in Memphis.

Radio station KLUE, in Longview, Texas, had sponsored an enormous public bonfire of Beatles memorabilia, and was knocked off the air the following day when a bolt of lightning struck its broadcast tower, burning out its equipment and rendering its news director unconscious. Little more need be said.

The year of the faux pas. Lennon angered fundamentalists with the assertion that the Beatles were 'more popular than Jesus Christ,' and Capitol created a hornet's nest—as well as a collector's item—by using the photo *below* on the *Yesterday and Today* album cover. It remains the essential piece of memorabilia in any Beatlemaniac's collection.

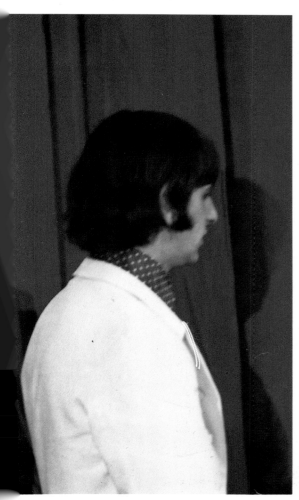

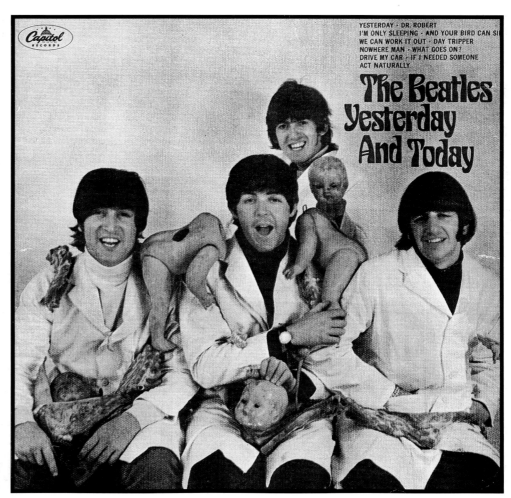

Above, from top to bottom: **Harrison with his sitar; Ravi Shankar, the Indian sitarist who became Harrison's teacher and lifelong friend; Lennon (as Private Gripweed) in a moment of angst during** *How I Won the War. Opposite:* **Klaus Voorman's intriguing cover art for the great turning point album, which was originally supposed to be called** *The Beatles On Safari.*

Aside from this flap, the Beatles' North American tour was a success, both in dollar terms and in terms of the enthusiastic response they'd received from their audiences. This tour covered fewer cities than the 1964 tour, but more than in 1965. As in 1965, Toronto was the only Canadian city on the tour. The Beatles also played Shea Stadium again, this time for two nights, with a record attendance for both nights.

When the Beatles left the stage after their concert at San Francisco's Candlestick Park on 29 August, few people, if any, realized that this would be the last formal concert that the Beatles would *ever* give before a paying audience. Brian Epstein was quoted as commenting privately that 'this will be the last Beatle concert ever,' and George Harrison said on the way home, 'Well, I guess that's it. I'm not a Beatle any more.'

San Francisco would be the end of an era that had begun with the first chords that touched off Beatlemania three years before. The screams died away that night and there would be no more to come. A 1967 tour would soon be in the planning stages but it would never happen. Nor would the elaborately planned 1969 tour.

At that time, the Beatles didn't have a specific intention to stop touring and playing live concerts, but neither did they have an overriding desire to see them continue. Within a few years—ironically, thanks to what was already taking place in 1966 in San Francisco—rock concerts would become an art form unto themselves. In the meantime, they had become, for the Beatles, just monstrous spectacles at which neither the musicians nor the fans could hear the music. How could playing such concerts compare to the creative pleasure derived from developing a work such as *Rubber Soul*?

With *Rubber Soul*, the Beatles had begun to experiment with sounds that could not be reproduced on stage with anything short of a 20-piece orchestra—nor was a stadium filled with 20,000 screaming fans an ideal setting to display the subtlety of their new music.

What had been true of *Rubber Soul* was doubly true of *Revolver*, which was released on 5 August in the United Kingdom and three days later in the United States. The songs chosen for the single that would be released in both countries from this album—*Yellow Submarine* and *Eleanor Rigby*—were masterpieces of Lennon/McCartney storytelling and Beatles musicianship. In the case of *Yellow Submarine*, the choice of Ringo Starr as singer was perfect for such a whimsical fantasy.

Revolver was truly a pioneering effort in terms of a 'concept' album, a style used by the Beatles and other groups in the late 1960s and early 1970s. The structure of this type of album, rather than simply being a collection of basically unrelated works gathered together in random order, features songs that are arranged to form an integrated, finished product (almost in classical style). The lyrics on *Revolver* ranged from the light sarcasm of *Dr Robert* to the biting irony of *Taxman*, and the music varied from the up-tempo, pop phrasing of *Good Day Sunshine*, to the musty strains of *Tomorrow Never Knows*, which seemed to have more in common with a Tibetan mantra than Elvis rockabilly. Indeed, one line *was* drawn from the *Tibetan Book of the Dead*. Although it has been widely rumored over the years that *Tomorrow Never Knows* was recorded under the working title *The Void*, the working title was, in fact, the far less mysterious *Mark I*.

Despite this remarkable eclecticism, *Revolver* functioned so well as a unit that, probably for the first time in pop music history, it was possible to look at an LP as a seamlessly complete work rather than as a haphazard selection of tunes. Despite its radical departure from the accepted norm, *Revolver* had little trouble scaling the *Billboard* chart within a month of its release.

With a fourth annual autumn tour of the United Kingdom canceled, the Beatles went their separate ways for two months–in what would, eventually, lead to a pattern of spending more of the year apart than together. Indeed, Brian Epstein would be faced with having to quell rumors that the Beatles were breaking up. Shorn of his Beatles haircut, John Lennon went south to Spain to play a non-singing dramatic role in *How I Won the War*. Directed by Richard Lester, the man who'd directed the two Beatles movies, this surreal comedy about World War II was released a year later, in October 1967.

George Harrison journeyed to India with his wife to study the *sitar* with Ravi Shankar, while Ringo Starr simply went on vacation. Meanwhile, Paul McCartney–who had been writing and producing for other groups since 1964–was commissioned to write the score for the film *The Family Way*, which would be recorded by an orchestra conducted by George Martin.

For both Parlophone and Capitol, the Beatles' pursuit of separate interests meant that there would be no album for pre-Christmas release as there had been in 1964 and 1965. The Beatles went back into the studio on 24 November and recorded several songs, but there was clearly not enough time for an album, so Parlophone released its first 'Beatles' greatest hits' album. Called simply *A Collection of Beatles Oldies*, it contained 16 tracks spanning the years from *She Loves You* to *Yellow Submarine*. In the United States, Capitol stood by as the Tony Sheridan sessions were repackaged and released on minor labels as part of two collections of miscellaneous artists.

It was a fitting end to a year of change that found the Beatles out of the public eye, yet in the studio. It was during the final weeks of 1966 that work began on what was to be the greatest album of their career.

SGT PEPPER'S LONELY HEARTS CLUB BAND

'They've been going in and out of style,
but they're guaranteed to raise a smile.'
–Sgt Pepper's Lonely Hearts Club Band
(1967)

The Beatles began 1967 with the abandonment of their touring career a foregone conclusion, although it was not 'officially' announced until October, when they rejected a million dollar offer for a one-night stand at Shea Stadium. The work on a new album to follow *Revolver*, which had begun in November 1966 at the Abbey Road Studios, continued into January 1967. Also during January, Brian Epstein succeeded in negotiating a new contract with EMI which increased the Beatles' royalties on their records from 10 to 17.5 percent. It would be worth millions and it would more than make up for any loss from not touring.

Meanwhile, two songs recorded during December were prepared for release as a single. Musically, these two songs represented a continuation of the vibrant complexity that differentiated their work since *Rubber Soul* from that of their earlier period. Indeed, the complexity of the work was now underscored by the fact that over 20 takes and overdubbings were now required for many of the tracks. The work now included not only elaborate sounds created by the Beatles themselves, but by as many as 40 session musicians from major orchestras, including the Royal Philharmonic and the London Symphony.

The lyrics to these two songs on the single were an autobiographical memoir of Beatles' bygone youth spent on the streets of Liverpool. *Penny Lane* was more than a Liverpool street; in the hands of Lennon and McCartney it became a

metaphor, a sometimes comical, often nostalgic kaleidoscope of images which defined the texture of the city of the Beatles' birth. The lyrics were peopled with a 'barber showing photographs of every head he's had the pleasure to have known'; a 'banker with a motor car' behind whose back children (including young John, Paul, George and Ringo) laughed; a 'fireman with an hour glass' holding a portrait of the Queen in his pocket as he shined the firetruck; a 'pretty nurse selling poppies from a tray'; and the people who 'come and go' and stop to say 'Hello.' Like the *I Feel Fine/She's A Woman* and *We Can Work It Out/Day Tripper* singles before it, *Penny Lane/Strawberry Fields* had two A sides–a double-sided hit. In the single's second A side, John Lennon invited listeners to let him take them to Strawberry Fields, the ancient and rundown estate where he had played as a child and where 'nothing is real and nothing to get hung about.'

The *Penny Lane/Strawberry Fields Forever* single was first aired on 31 January, on BBC radio in England, and on 2 February in the United States. Released two weeks later worldwide, it had reached number three on the *Melody Maker* charts by 25 February, and was number one on 4 March.

In January, meanwhile, the Beatles had recorded a 14-minute audio collage for the *Carnival of Light* at the London Roundhouse Theater. Produced under Paul McCartney's direction, the

Right: Let them take you down. Any similarity between Sgt Pepper's Lonely Hearts Club Band and the band that had been known as the Beatles was purely coincidental.

piece was similar to *Revolution 9*, which the group would record in 1968, and was characterized by many of the unorthodox techniques–such as reversed tape, multiple overdubs and electronic sound–that they were now using in the songs like *Strawberry Fields Forever*. The *Carnival of Light* soundtrack was aired at the Roundhouse as planned but never heard publicly again.

On 30 March, with Ringo on lead vocal, the Beatles recorded (*I Get By) With a Little Help From My Friends*. This would be the last song of a four-month session that began with *Penny Lane* and ultimately produced the material for the album considered by many fans and rock historians alike as the Beatles' best. *Sgt Pepper's Lonely Hearts Club Band* would be a significant album in more ways than one.

The centerpiece for the cover photo was a bass drum elaborately painted with the logo of the fictional lonely hearts club band, which the equally fictitious sergeant had taught to play '20 years ago today.' The Beatles stood behind the bass drum dressed in brilliantly colored Victorian band costumes, surrounded by photographic cutouts and mannequins representing famous (and infamous) personalities. To their right were wax figures of themselves dressed in the dark suits in which they had

performed at concerts a few years before. The wax figures underscored the contrast between the Beatles of 1967 and the Beatles of 1965.

The Beatles were on the leading edge of a wave of change that was sweeping the popular music world–and it was a tidal wave. Released on 1 June 1967, *Sgt Pepper's Lonely Hearts Club Band* not only was a milestone for the Beatles, but it also became a symbol of 1967–the year the tidal wave struck–a year which itself is regarded as a landmark in popular music history. Twenty years later, the 'sixties' are still seen as a mother lode of important popular music, which begat an unprecedented explosion of creative output that was felt in every corner of the globe.

The 'sixties,' as a musical era, can be defined by the musicians and musical groups in their heyday then, just as the Renaissance era is defined by *its* great artists and composers. When one lists the musicians and musical groups by which the 'sixties' are defined, one almost invariably finds that 1967 was the year these performers either released their first album or reached the pinnacle of lasting stardom.

There seems to have been two epicenters of this 'sixties sound.' In London, of the groups that had been formed on the coattails of the Beatles, only the best–such as the Rolling Stones and The Who–survived. Most notably, there were the groups which formed around guitarists, such as Eric Clapton and Peter Green, who were alumni of a little-known club band called John May-

Below: **Sgt Pepper's band at EMI's Abbey Road studios, and** (*facing page*) **their landmark album. The incredibly expensive jacket photo was designed by British pop artists Peter Blake and Jan Haworth.**

all's Bluesbreakers. Eric Clapton joined Jack Bruce and Ginger Baker to form Cream, and Peter Green joined Mick Fleetwood in the seminal configuration of a band that has lasted one-quarter of a century: Fleetwood Mac.

Half a world away, in San Francisco, the local concert scene tapped a vein of talent unparalleled in rock history. By early 1967, two small concert halls–Bill Graham's Fillmore Auditorium and the Avalon Ballroom, operated by Chet Helms' Family Dog Productions–were offering a smorgasbord of emerging talent which was so outstanding that, today, it almost seems impossible it could have happened so quickly, all in one place. But it did.

The San Francisco 'sound' was just beginning to evolve at the time of the Beatles' last concert there, in August 1966, and, indeed, many of the people who later would create the San Francisco 'sound' were *at* that show. By the following spring, that sound was audible at the Fillmore and the Avalon. It was heard in the music of the Jefferson Airplane, the Grateful Dead,

Quicksilver Messenger Service and a band with the improbable name 'Big Brother And The Holding Company,' which featured not a big brother, but a female vocalist named Janis Joplin, who is one of that handful of singers by whom the 'sixties' would come to be defined.

The music was, however, only one component of the tidal wave. The whole socio-cultural fabric of Western civilization was being changed–in both subtle and overt ways–by the generation of people who had come of age in the era of the Beatles. There were moral, ethical and philosophical changes afoot in the late 1960s that will be studied and analyzed for decades to come. The spark that was somehow struck–on the corner of Haight and Ashbury Streets in San Francisco during the summer of 1967–shocked, then consumed, the Western world. What took shape in the space of a few short months on that street corner, and at the Monterey Pop Festival (which was co-produced by former Brian Epstein assistant Derek Taylor), *and* at the Human Be-In in San Francisco's Golden Gate Park, was nothing short of the

genesis of an alternate society that would become known as 'the counterculture,' until it merged with mainstream society–forever changing it–a decade or so later.

There was an excitement and electricity to the counterculture during that pivotal summer in San Francisco which is hard to define. It was probably very much like being around on the day that someone first discovered fire. Within this alternate society, 'peace' and 'love' were the stated ideals (the summer of '67 was even called the 'summer of love'); the hallucinogenic drug LSD was its 'sacrament;' *Sgt Pepper* was its bible; and the Beatles and Bob Dylan were among its pantheon of deities.

To think of a drug as 'sacramental' seems today as absurd as it was to 'establishment' people in 1967. To discuss it at all in the present is *only* to examine its role in the thinking that went into the making of *Sgt Pepper*.

The use of hallucinogenic, or psychedelic, drugs dates back thousands of years and is intertwined with the religious experiences of many cultures throughout the world. The visions recorded by holy men down through history–from medieval Europe to Vedic India–parallel those conjured up by hallucinogenic drugs used during the 'summer of love.' When LSD (lysergic acid diethylamide) was synthesized by Sandoz Pharmaceuticals in Switzerland in the 1950s, it was discovered that its effects were very much like that of the mescaline in peyote cactus and psilocybin in the mushrooms used for centuries by the Indians of the American Southwest.

In his 1954 book, *The Doors of Perception*, Aldous Huxley described his own experience with mescaline. Reporting 90 minutes after taking the drug, he writes:

'[I] was sitting in my study, looking intently at a small glass vase. The vase contained only three flowers–a full-blown Belle of Portugal rose, shell pink with a hint at every petal's base of a hotter, flamier hue; a large magenta- and cream-colored carnation; and, pale purple at the end of its broken stalk, the bold, heraldic blossom of an iris. Fortuitous and provisional, the little nosegay broke all the rules of traditional good taste. At breakfast

The 'Sixties Pantheon' (American section) was led by Bob Dylan, the surrealistic poet folk singer (*top left* in a 1978 appearance) whose lyrics–influenced by everyone from Rimbaud to Woody Guthrie–inspired a generation. The epicenter of the American scene was the 'San Francisco sound,' typified by (*clockwise from top right*) Jefferson Airplane, Janis Joplin and the Grateful Dead. Other important figures of this era included Jimi Hendrix, the Byrds and the Doors.

that morning I had been struck by the lively dissonance of its colors. But that was no longer the point. I was not looking now at an unusual flower arrangement. I was seeing what Adam had seen on the morning of his creation–the miracle, moment by moment, of naked existence.

'As Mind at Large seeps past the no longer watertight valve, all kinds of biologically useless things start to happen. In some cases there may be extra-sensory perceptions. Other persons discover a world of visionary beauty. To others again is revealed the glory, the infinite value and meaningfulness of naked existence, of the given, unconceptualized event. In the final stage of egolessness there is an "obscure knowledge" that All is in all–that All is actually each. This is as near, I take it, as a finite mind can ever come to "perceiving everything that is happening everywhere in the universe." '

LSD remained an obscure experience, available to only a very few, until it suddenly came into wide circulation in 1967 from a clandestine factory in San Francisco. John Lennon and George Harrison, however, had actually first had their experience with LSD in early 1965, when a dentist friend–reportedly Dr Charles Robert of New York–had secretly dosed their coffee at a London dinner party. It was an experience that Lennon later discussed wryly in the song *Dr Robert*. 'Take a drink from his special cup,' wrote Lennon. 'He helps you understand, he does everything he can.'

Lennon continued his psychedelic experiences with subsequent voluntary acid trips. The fact that his own psychic 'discoveries' paralleled Huxley's is evident in the songs such as *She Said She Said* and *Tomorrow Never Knows* from the *Revolver* album. 'Turn off your mind, relax and float down stream,' he wrote in the latter. 'Lay down all thought, surrender to the void…it is shining…That you may see the meaning of within…it is knowing.'

How the psychedelic experience affected the Beatles' music has been the subject of wide debate. Certainly it had *some* effect. The complexity and diversity of *Rubber Soul* and *Revolver* can,

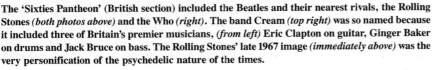

The 'Sixties Pantheon' (British section) included the Beatles and their nearest rivals, the Rolling Stones (*both photos above*) and the Who (*right*). The band Cream (*top right*) was so named because it included three of Britain's premier musicians, (*from left*) Eric Clapton on guitar, Ginger Baker on drums and Jack Bruce on bass. The Rolling Stones' late 1967 image (*immediately above*) was the very personification of the psychedelic nature of the times.

in some part, be traced to the fact that they were recorded *after* John and George first took LSD. However, Paul McCartney did *not* allow himself to be talked into taking LSD until early 1967 during the *Sgt Pepper* sessions. There may or may not be a connection between the fact that this album, considered their finest, was produced at a time when all the Beatles were actively taking LSD.

One song from the album, *Lucy in the Sky with Diamonds*, was undisguised psychedelic literature–even its initials were LSD! John Lennon, however, always said this was a coincidence and that the title was inspired by a drawing by his three-year-old son Julian. In it, Lennon and McCartney wrote: 'Picture yourself in a boat on a river, with tangerine trees and marmalade skies. Somebody calls you, you answer quite slowly, a girl with kaleidoscope eyes.' The girl is, of course, Lucy, and her message was quite clear.

A Day in the Life, the closing song on the *Sgt Pepper* album, was criticized (and banned from BBC radio) for being an encouragement for youth to become involved with drugs because of the line 'I'd love to turn you on.' Tracing its subject through either a day of his lifetime or a lifetime of many dimensions, the song is, in fact, an intricate symbolic epic that could fit comfortably on a shelf between *Beowulf* and *Sad Eyed Lady of the Lowlands*.

George Harrison's composition from the album was less overt and in it he meshed the psychedelic experience with Eastern mysticism against the appropriately conceived musical background of his sitar. In *Within You Without You* he wrote about the 'space between us all and the people who hide themselves behind a wall of illusion,' and he went on to remind listeners that 'life flows on within you and without you.'

Because of all the mysticism read into the album by an entire generation that was listening to it while on LSD, some fairly light-hearted songs took on a peculiar significance. John Lennon adapted the lyrics of *Being for the Benefit of Mr Kite* from the text of an old circus poster, but a great many people invested a tremendous amount of time trying to decipher the 'secret' meaning behind this mysterious 'Mr Kite,' his trampoline and his waltzing horse.

Of the album's serious songs, *She's Leaving Home* became the anthem of a generation of young, disaffected people abandoning the mainstream culture, represented by their parents, for the mythic 'freedom' represented by the San Francisco counterculture. In this carefully crafted song, Paul McCartney cleverly inserted cliched parental dialogue into parentheses as counterpoint to his narration: 'She (What did we do that was wrong) is leaving (We didn't know it was wrong) home (Fun is the one

Above: George Harrison and Derek Taylor flew into San Francisco in August 1967 to visit Haight Street and savor the Summer of Love. *Right:* Sgt Pepper's band in full uniform on stage at London's Saville Theatre on 10 November 1967 filming promo 'video' for *Hello Goodbye*. Compare this photo to the ones on pages 36 and 37.

thing that money can't buy) something inside that was always denied for so many years…She's leaving home…bye bye.'

Having ended their public career in San Francisco a year before the 'summer of love,' the Beatles made no fourth annual visit to 'The City by the Golden Gate.' What would have happened, during a period when the Beatles were actually deified, if they had played even one concert at the Fillmore that summer has been the subject of many a fond fantasy. Paul McCartney had visited San Francisco immediately after *Sgt Pepper* was finished. On 4 April he attended a rehearsal of the Jefferson Airplane at their big Victorian mansion on Fulton Street adjacent to Golden Gate Park, but he made no public appearances and quietly slipped away the following day.

It was clear, from this point on, that the counterculture was a global phenomenon, but no one–not even John Lennon and Paul McCartney–could predict how far reaching it would soon become. When they wrote *All You Need Is Love* in May, it was conceived as a commentary on the times, but when it was released (on 7 July in England and 17 July in the United States) it helped turn the 'summer of love' from a San Francisco event into a worldwide state of mind.

George Harrison was the only Beatle to visit the Haight-Ashbury district during that mythical summer. Wearing shoulder-length hair, heart-shaped sunglasses and carrying an acoustic guitar, he was hardly out of place when he wandered through Golden Gate Park and began strolling down Haight Street on 8 August. Once recognized, George paused briefly to provide the amazed fans with an impromptu serenade.

It was a brief moment in a brief and brilliant summer. The spontaneity of the moment could not, by definition, last forever–and indeed, it did not survive the summer. The summer ended, but the changes wrought by it remained. The face of the music and the culture would be forever altered by those who had looked past, and stepped beyond, the 'doors of perception.' They had learned a new kind of innovation, and they had learned to see with different eyes, and they moved on to share their message with the world. For those who *remained* beyond the doors, however, there was a gathering darkness. The means had become an end. For the Beatles, the ugliest downside of drugs was soon to become very apparent within their own family.

With no tours to plan, and with the Beatles themselves officially committed to but one album per year, Brian Epstein suddenly had a very empty life. His family business, NEMS, had gone from being a chain of music stores to a major entertainment empire. He'd managed other groups like The Cyrkle and entertainers like Cilla Black, but the Beatles were the centerpiece of NEMS and the focal point of Epstein's life. The role played by pills–both uppers and downers–in that lonely life, increased. Depression led to drug dependency, which only served to feed the monster of depression.

The last weekend in August was a three day bank holiday. The Beatles had last seen Epstein on the preceding Wednesday during the recording session for *Your Mother Should Know*, and on Friday they had gone to Bangor, in Wales, to attend a meditation lecture given by the Maharishi Mahesh Yogi–a Hindu holy man with an international following. Brian Epstein had gone to his country home in Sussex with two friends, but had returned to London without explanation late Friday night. When he telephoned his houseguests on Saturday to apologize for not staying on, he sounded groggy. The following day, 27 August, Brian Epstein was found dead of an overdose of a sleeping potion called Carbitol in his London home.

The Beatles were left unexpectedly with the entire burden of managing a multimillion dollar empire, whose full extent they did not comprehend. The only man who *had* understood the elaborate intricacies of the Beatles' global tangle of contracts and commitments in publishing and recording was now dead. There was no heir apparent. Clive Epstein replaced his brother as chairman of NEMS, but he felt immediately overwhelmed, and he was ultimately ineffective and unable to fill Brian's shoes. Paul McCartney described Clive as being like a 'provincial furniture salesman.'

The Beatles were left holding the bag. For all their creative brilliance, none of them had ever *managed* so much as a personal checkbook, much less a business of such awesome proportions. They had, in fact, spent their entire adult lives *being* managed. Now, they had been snatched from the insulated netherworld of recording studios, alternative realities and blissful fantasies and were thrust into the icy waters of reality.

On one hand they had all the money they could use–and that would buy some time to get organized–but on the other hand, they were victims of a momentum of their own creation. The larger-than-life entity known as 'the Beatles' had taken on a life of its own that superseded and overshadowed the individual lives of John, Paul, George and Ringo. Without Brian Epstein to control and direct it, this entity was like an automobile without a driver careening down a highway at high speed.

On 1 September, three days after Brian Epstein's funeral, the four still shaken Beatles sat down to decide how to proceed with their various projects. Work on the animated film based on the 1966 song *Yellow Submarine* had begun in June, but it was mainly in the hands of the animators. Thus, there was little hands-on work for the Beatles themselves, until the project reached a more advanced state of completion and they would be needed to record additional songs for the soundtrack. A planned trip to India to visit the Maharishi Mahesh Yogi, planned for September, was postponed until February, so the decision was made to proceed immediately with Paul McCartney's idea for *another* film.

Conceived by Paul in April while he was flying home from his visit to the United States, the film would be called *Magical Mystery Tour*. It would be a comedic farce in which the Beatles and an unusual collection of hangers-on and carnival sideshow people travel about the English countryside in a large touring bus, becoming involved in various humorously related misadventures. The 'bus' portion of filming for the tour began in Cornwall on 11 September and lasted only two days. Filming

Above: **Ringo and Paul, on the Magical Mystery Tour, as two of the Five Magicians whose spell spirit the bus away to the amazing musical land of the walrus, and** *below* **with John and George as part of the band.**

continued at an air base in West Malling and in other locations, and the Beatles were back in EMI's Abbey Road studios by 25 September ready to start work on the song *The Fool on the Hill*, which would figure prominently in the film's soundtrack.

In the meantime, the Beatles had made the decision to start a company–actually a *group* of companies–which would be known as 'Apple.' The idea was that the Beatles would have a network of interests that paralleled those which Brian Epstein had in NEMS. In September, Apple Publishing was founded to handle music publishing, but, ironically, the Lennon-McCartney songs were still associated with Northern Songs, and hence, would not be available to the new venture. Another unrelated company, Apple Electronics, was established at the same time to handle the patents on the creations of the eccentric Greek inventor Alexis 'Magic Alex' Mardas. In February 1968

The tour includes lunch, while the band plays a Spanish dance, a brief visit with the military and for George and John (*above*), along with the rest of the men, a stop at a striptease club.

'Apple' would become Apple Corps Ltd, an extremely diverse, and ultimately unsuccessful, holding company.

Between 22 August and 5 November, the Beatles recorded a number of versions of five new Lennon-McCartney songs, as well as George Harrison's *Blue Jay Way* (written on a foggy night in early August on the street in the Hollywood hills of the same name). Also recorded was an intriguing instrumental called *Flying* (working title: *Aerial Tour*), which was the first of only two songs ever credited to all four Beatles.

Four of the Lennon-McCartney songs were planned for incorporation into the *Magical Mystery Tour* film. These were *The Fool on the Hill*, (*Though she was born a long, long time ago*) *Your Mother Should Know*, *I Am the Walrus*, and the film's title track. The last song, *Hello Goodbye*, was not in the film but released by Parlophone on 24 November as a single with *I Am the Walrus* backing it. Three days later, Capitol released the single, along with a *Magical Mystery Tour* 'soundtrack' album that included all six of the songs from the film, as well as *Hello Goodbye*, *Penny Lane*, *Strawberry Fields Forever*, *Baby You're a Rich Man* and *All You Need Is Love*. On 8 December Parlophone released the six film songs only on a two-disc, seven-inch, extended-play (EP) album.

Reaction to the songs was generally good. The single went to number one and the others were generally on par with those from *Sgt Pepper*, although, as a package, they lacked the coherence of the preceding three albums. Paul McCartney's *Your Mother Should Know* was itself 'guaranteed to raise a smile.' At the same time, John Lennon's *I Am the Walrus* gave the fans who saw his work as a musical cryptogram plenty to chew on, with characters like 'crabalocker fishwife,' 'elementary penguin,' 'pornographic priestess' and 'the eggman,' as well as with lines such as 'See how they fly, like Lucy in the sky, see how they run.'

Paul McCartney's *The Fool on the Hill* demonstrated *his* ability to craft thought-provoking lyrics. Although the identity of the 'fool' was never satisfactorily named, clues remain: 'Day after day, alone on a hill, the man with the foolish grin is keeping perfectly still. But nobody wants to know him, they can see that he's just a fool, and he never gives an answer. But the fool on the hill sees the sun going down and the eyes in his head see the world spinning round.'

The long-awaited *Magical Mystery Tour* film itself was not premiered until the day after Christmas. Being only 54 minutes long, it was too short for theatrical release, and having been turned down by the American networks, it wound up being broadcast on BBC TV in black and white rather than color. The reaction of the public to the film was the most negative of any that the Beatles had received to any of their projects. Those who were hoping for another *Hard Day's Night* or *Help!* were bitterly disappointed. *Magical Mystery Tour* was essentially a succession of what we know today as 'rock videos' with little or no unifying theme or plot, despite the two-day bus trip.

The year 1967 was pivotal for the Beatles. In the first full year of their career with no public concerts, they had come 'back into style' in the persona of 'Sgt Pepper's Lonely Hearts Club Band,' and had released an album which was hailed not only as the milestone of their career, but as a milestone in recording industry history as well. They stepped out of this persona to follow the Maharishi Mahesh Yogi on the eve of Brian Epstein's death, and soon their magical mystery tour had taken them to a rendezvous with the most sour note they'd yet known.

It was the loss of Brian Epstein, however, that would ultimately be remembered as the cruelest blow–and the one whose impact would be felt the hardest in the coming years.

1968

WE CAN WORK IT OUT

'Hey Jude, you'll do. The movement you need is on your shoulder. Hey Jude, don't make it bad, take a sad song and make it better; remember to let her under your skin, then you'll begin to make it better.'
–John Lennon and Paul McCartney (1968)

The death of Brian Epstein in August 1967 was not just a severe personal loss for John Lennon, Paul McCartney, George Harrison and Ringo Starr. For them collectively, in the context of the entity called 'The Beatles,' Epstein's demise was the beginning of the end. The relationship between Brian Epstein and the Beatles had been a symbiotic one. They created the sound that made Beatlemania possible, but he managed and modulated the phenomena, and in the process, made all five of them rich. So after they finished their road work and sequestered themselves in a studio, Epstein felt his life begin to lose its purpose. True, the enormous creative momentum inherent in this unique partnership remained. Indeed, much of the Beatles' best work still lay ahead, but the cohesiveness–that had begun to erode as early as 1966–continued to gradually slip away.

Apple had potential that was beyond belief. A multimedia, multinational holding company–which included the Beatles, and which was now a beacon for many very talented people from all over the world–was a one in a million opportunity. It was a chance that would have been tailor-made for Brian Epstein–had he lived to help it grow. Apple was an entity that begged for a Brian Epstein, but none was available. The Beatles served only as Apple's figureheads; they were never available for day-to-day management, and hence abdicated any possible role as anything other than figureheads.

'Apple' the idea became Apple the company in February 1968, when the partnership known as The Beatles, Ltd (established in June 1963) officially changed its name to Apple Corps, Ltd. Under this new umbrella, the Beatles assembled their potpourri of smaller Apples, such as Apple Electronics and Apple Publishing–which had existed since the previous September–as well

as Apple Retail, which was itself an umbrella for the two-month-old Apple Boutique, an exotic emporium of clothing and baubles which opened amid high hopes at 94 Baker Street in London on 7 December. Two new ventures that would garner the most attention in the coming months were Apple Records and Apple Films. The former was conceived as an all-new record company under which the Beatles would find and develop new talent in the form of new groups and solo performers. The Beatles themselves had existing contracts with EMI and Capitol, and thus could not record for their own company. However, an arrangement was worked out whereby future Beatles records would carry Apple *labels* but would be *distributed* by EMI and Capitol, and they would carry Parlophone and Capitol serial numbers. EMI and Capitol would also help distribute other Apple products.

Apple Films was much the same as Apple Records in theory. The plan was for it to serve as the financial and production vehicle for any film project that the Beatles (individually and collectively) decided to undertake, as well as any other film project any of them might support. The first project inherited by this division was the feature length animated film based on the 1966 Lennon-McCartney song, *Yellow Submarine*. Directed overall by George Dunning, the animation was done in Holland during the summer of 1967 under the direction of Heinz Edelmann. *Yellow Submarine* was nearing completion in February 1968 when the Beatles went into the studio to record four new songs for the soundtrack. Scheduled for a May release, *Yellow Submarine* did not actually premier in London until July, and not until November in the United States.

It was also during this time that Paul McCartney's *Step Inside Love* and *Lady Madonna* were recorded, the latter to appear in

The Beatles' first album on their own Apple label *(above)* was released amid a great flurry of optimism and excitement about the future. Throughout most of 1968, it seemed as though the dream really would come true.

March as the A side of the next Beatles single. This single would be the last Beatles release on the Parlophone and Capitol labels before their transition to the Apple label.

On 16 February John and Cynthia Lennon, along with George Harrison, his wife, Pattie, and her sister Jenny Boyd, left London and the seedling Apple Corps to fly to the Maharishi Mahesh Yogi's meditation retreat in Rishikesh, India. They were joined three days later by Ringo and his wife, Maureen, along with Paul McCartney and his long-time girlfriend, Jane Asher. What was intended to be a two-month long meditation course for the Beatles turned into a media event and resulted in their general disillusionment with the grinning guru.

Ringo and Maureen left after only two weeks, describing it as being like summer camp with overspiced food. Paul and Jane departed on 26 March, followed by John, George and their entourage at the end of April. Though the original purpose of the trip was unsuccessful due to their falling out with the Maharishi, the Beatles were able to get some well-earned rest, and used the time to write the songs for their next album, which subsequently would be recorded over the summer and released in the fall.

While they were abroad, *Lady Madonna* was released, backed with *The Inner Light*. This song had lyrics adapted by Geroge Harrison almost verbatim from the *Tao Te Ching*. It featured George's vocals accompanied by an instrumental track that he had recorded with traditional Indian musicians at EMI's studio in Bombay in January while he was also working on the soundtrack for the film, *Wonderwall*.

With the Beatles out of touch for over a month during the critical early days of Apple Corps, the task of overall management fell to its director, Neil Aspinall. He had been the Beatles' road manager—when they were *still* on the road—and had helped Brian Epstein manage and arrange all their tours. Derek Taylor, press agent to the Beatles prior to a 1964 falling out with Brian Epstein, rejoined them in March as head of publicity for Apple Corps. Mal Evans, Aspinall's assistant since 1963, was named as general manager for the Apple Records division. Very soon after the headquarters of Apple Corps was selected at 95 Wigmore Street in London, the new company was deluged by artists and musicians wanting to be part of the magical mystery of the creative empire founded by the Beatles.

On 11 May Neil Aspinall and Derek Taylor flew to New York, along with John Lennon and Paul McCartney, for a series of press conferences and other appearances, including a 15 May spot on NBC-TV's *Tonight Show*, to officially promote Apple Corps in the American media. Meanwhile, George Harrison and Ringo Starr, together with their wives, flew to the south of France for the 17 May premier of *Wonderwall* at the Cannes Film Festival.

The sore spot in the Apple Corps empire continued to be the retail division—specifically, the Apple Boutique on Baker Street. Long a victim of supplier pilferage and the general anti-materialistic tenor of the times, the Apple Boutique had become a horrible money drain, and on 30 July Paul McCartney announced its closing. The following day, after two frenzied days of literally giving away the store's entire inventory to hordes of eager bargain seekers, the Boutique became a thing of the past.

By this time, the rest of Apple Corps had actually taken on some life and momentum. This seemed to buoy the enthusiasm of the Beatles, who had previously appeared apathetic to their

Only a block from tony Regent Street, 3 Savile Row *(at left in photo)* was the epicenter of Apple's 'magic kingdom' in 1968. But the magic was short-lived– Apple's golden age lasted less than six months.

own venture. The structure was finally in place for the Beatles to begin acting upon their creative dreams, and so was the money. The Beatles Ltd (now Apple Corps, Ltd) had netted well over £1 million pounds since the beginning of the year. The period from May through October 1968 represented the lamentably short-lived halcyon days of Apple Corps. During this period the Beatles (especially Paul, who was now taking more of an interest in the business aspects of Apple), actually came into the Apple Corps offices–which were moved to 3 Savile Row in August–nearly every weekday, and all of them (save Ringo) showed up for the 17 July premier of *Yellow Submarine* at London's Pavilion Theatre.

Simultaneously, much of their time was devoted to developing the new acts that had been signed by Apple Records. George Harrison began working with Jackie Lomax, while Paul took a variety of acts under his wing, including James Taylor and Mary Hopkin. For the latter's *Those Were the Days* single and album, Paul not only produced, he played most of the instruments. Even the Modern Jazz Quartet was lured aboard Apple for one album that would be released in December.

For the Beatles themselves, the summer of 1968 marked the most prolific–and in many ways the most creative–period of their career as a band. Well over 30 entirely new songs were recorded–enough for three albums–which would ultimately be edited down to a two-disc album and a single.

For John Lennon and Paul McCartney it was also a period of great change in their personal lives. With John, it was the end of his six-year marriage to Cynthia, while Paul's relationship with Jane Asher, which dated back almost as long, was being supplanted by his fascination for the American photographer Linda Eastman.

John had married Cynthia Powell in August 1962, eight months before the birth of their son, Julian. Like the relationship between John's parents, Alfred and Julia, John's family life with Cynthia and Julian was marked by long periods of separation. Alfred had run away to sea, and John was almost constantly on the road until Julian was three years old. Even after the Beatles stopped touring, John was hardly a homebody and was not entirely faithful to Cynthia.

The pivotal change in John Lennon's love life came in November 1966, when he met Japanese conceptual artist Yoko Ono at an exhibition of her work at the Indica Gallery in London. John was immediately taken by both her unusual sense of humor, which strongly dovetailed with his own, and her concept of art, which was a synthesis of styles inspired by the work of John Cage and Isamu Noguchi, who had drawn their inspiration from the Zen culture of her native Japan. Her art, in which the *idea* was all important and the technique almost irrelevant, was, and still is, hard for most people to understand–and hence, is far less appealing to the general public. The fact that John understood her certainly contributed to Yoko's attraction to him. They saw each other occasionally over the ensuing years, but it was not until May 1968 that a serious romance began to take shape.

It was also during May that their first joint art exhibit opened at the Arts Lab in London. Though John's affair with Yoko was well known by this time, Cynthia would not actually sue for divorce until 22 August. On 8 November, the day the divorce was granted, Cynthia was alone in the courtroom. John was at Yoko's bedside in Queen Charlotte's Hospital, where she faced the miscarriage of their first child which, in fact, did take place on November 12.

Paul McCartney's affair with Jane Asher dated back to May 1963, when Jane was 17, and when she met Paul after the Beatles' Royal Albert Hall concert. Soon after, Paul moved into

In the 1968 film *Yellow Submarine*, the submarine itself visited dowdy Liverpool *(facing page top)* to whisk the Beatles away to 'Pepperland' where–under the guise of Sgt Pepper's band–they defeated the 'Blue Meanies' and restored color and happiness by chanting their 1967 mantra *(facing page bottom)*.

Jane's parents' home, where he remained until late 1966, when he finally bought his own house. During this time, Jane's mother became almost a surrogate parent for Paul (whose own mother died when he was a teenager), and Paul wrote a great many songs for Jane's brother Peter, and his partner Gordon Waller, whose duo–Peter & Gordon–was a successful act on the British pop charts in the mid-1960s. Among other songs, Paul wrote Peter & Gordon's biggest hit, *A World Without Love*–a song whose release coincided with the Beatles' initial burst of worldwide success in 1964.

A marriage between Paul McCartney and Jane Asher was rumored to be in the offing–or to have actually happened–numerous times over the years. Jane was frequently at his side in London and around the world, and though he never denied his *intention* to one day marry her, Paul seemed to be in no mad rush to the altar. Their engagement was, in fact, not officially announced until Christmas 1967, and she accompanied him to India in February 1968.

Meanwhile, however, Paul had met Linda Louise Eastman, an aspiring rock photographer born in Scarsdale, New York, who was four years older than Jane and three months younger than he. She was also the mother of a six-year-old daughter. They met a second time in New York, during John and Paul's May 1968 visit to promote Apple Corps, and they stayed in touch thereafter. When Paul visited Los Angeles in late June, they spent four days together in a bungalow at the Beverly Hills Hotel. A month later Jane Asher announced that her engagement to Paul

Above: John Lennon and Yoko Ono at a gallery opening in 1968, the year their affair turned serious. *Right:* EMI's studio on Abbey Road where the Beatles five-month recording session in mid-1968 produced the almost mythical 'White Album.'

McCartney was off, although it would not be until October that Paul and Linda actually began living together.

There is little wonder that one of the most creative periods in Beatles history coincided with John Lennon and Paul McCartney both finding the lovers who would last, in John's case a lifetime, and in Paul's case, at least two decades. However, these two women also exerted more control over the artistic sides of their men's careers than had their predecessors, and are still seen by many as being contributing factors to the demise of the Lennon-McCartney friendship/partnership, as well as that of the Beatles. The political impact of Yoko Ono and Linda Eastman upon the Beatles would evolve over time, but in the summer of 1968 nearly everything was going right.

The triumphant climax of Apple Corps' summer activities came on 26 August with the simultaneous release in the United States of the first four Apple Records singles. In order of their serial numbers they were:

(a) *Thingamybob* b/w *Yellow Submarine* by John Foster & Sons, Ltd Black Dyke Mills Band.
(b) *Those Were the Days* b/w *Turn! Turn! Turn!* by Mary Hopkin.
(c) *Sour Milk Sea* b/w *The Eagle Laughs at You* by Jackie Lomax.
(d) *Hey Jude* b/w *Revolution* by the Beatles.

(The Mary Hopkin and Beatles singles were released in the United Kingdom four days later, and the others on 6 September. Mary Hopkin's single was recorded in four other languages and was released worldwide.)

The reaction to the Beatles' single was outstanding. Despite the fact that *Hey Jude* was over seven minutes long (double the length of an average single), it received very extensive airplay, entering the British and Dutch charts at number one and going to number one on the American charts by its second week. An incredible two million copies of *Hey Jude* were sold in the first two weeks, demonstrating that the genius and talent of the Beatles still clearly inspired a vast popular following five years after the birth of Beatlemania.

The 'take a sad song and make it better' optimism of *Hey Jude*

was as obviously appealing as John Lennon's lyrics for *Revolution* were controversial. While the summer of 1968 was marked by productivity and good fortune for the Beatles in London, other world cities were being rocked by political upheaval. In Paris, a student revolt turned into a general strike, which in turn brought the government down. In Prague, hundreds lay dead in the wake of a brutal Soviet invasion, while in Chicago, protests against American involvement in the Vietnam War turned into bloody riots at the Democratic Party's National Convention. It was the summer that the counterculture spawned in 1967 began to clash violently with the establishment. The 'summer of love' gave way to the summer of violent confrontation. *All You Need Is Love* was supplanted by *Revolution* as the anthem of the times.

John Lennon had become more outspoken about politics than most people in the rock music field. He frequently expressed a negative view of the American role in Vietnam and had generally taken the radical side of many controversial issues. It was a trend that would continue for him for the next four years, with *Revolution* being only the first of many overtly political songs. 'You say you want a revolution,' he said, addressing the global radical community which looked to someone like him for moral support.

The message he gave them, however, was tempered with moderation: 'We all want to change the world; but when you talk about destruction, don't you know that you can count me out?' The song also acknowledged his financial support for radical causes, but again added a temperate note: 'But if you want money for minds that hate, all I can tell you is brother you'll have to wait.' Ironically, *Revolution* ended on the same note as *Hey Jude* with the line, 'Don't you know it's going to be all right.'

To help promote a record that appeared to need no promoting, the Beatles agreed to play their first 'concert' before an audience in over two years. Held on 4 September, it wasn't so much a concert as it was a television taping with a live audience. It was, however, a nostalgic reminder of Beatles magic at work on a small crowd, a scene they hadn't played since they'd begun doing stadium-sized shows in 1964. The playlist ranged from *Hang Down Your Head, Tom Dooley* to *Hey Jude*. Of course the taping of the latter for broadcast five days later was the reason for the session.

The success of the other Apple releases certainly paled by comparison to those by the Beatles, although *Those Were the Days* did reach number one on the *Melody Maker* charts in October. Its sales certainly did benefit by the personal interest that Paul McCartney took in promoting both the record and Mary Hopkin. He even arranged for her to make television appearances on the *Ed Sullivan Show* in the United States, and on the *David Frost Show* in England.

The August release of the four Apple singles was followed in November by the release of the first three albums on the Apple label. The first of these, on 1 November, contained George Harrison's sitar-spangled soundtrack for the film *Wonderwall*. George's 'solo' release was followed on 11 November by a John Lennon/Yoko Ono album called *Unfinished Music I: Two Virgins*. It was a strange collection of unintelligible mumblings and ambient noise that John and Yoko had produced at home. Critics considered it a joke or an eccentric lark. The American distribution of *Wonderwall* was automatically undertaken by Capitol, but they refused to have anything to do with *Two Virgins* because of the jacket, which featured a black and white photo of John and Yoko–completely nude! Wrapped in brown paper, the album was finally distributed by Tetragrammaton.

The crowning achievement of the year for Apple, however, was the release of the LP which was called *The Beatles*,

Above: John Lennon with Paul McCartney's sheep dog Martha. *Right:* An advertisement for the untitled two-record album, which will forever be known simply as 'The White Album.'

but which will forever be known simply as 'The White Album.'

Issued on 22 November in the United Kingdom and on 25 November in the United States, it was a two-record set with an absolutely white jacket. The only features on its surface were a limited edition serial number (a different serial stamped on every album) and the legend 'The Beatles' embossed on the front. At first hearing, it seemed to lack the thematic unity of *Rubber Soul*, *Revolver* and *Sgt Pepper*, yet time showed it to be the richest and most diverse single work ever produced by the Beatles. It was their *magnum opus*.

With 30 songs covering a vast spectrum of styles and themes, 'The White Album' was actually *several* albums superimposed upon one another like the planes of a three dimensional chess board. It *opened* with a song that was pure rock-and-roll and yet, simultaneously, was a brilliant parody of rock-and-roll. It *closed* with a juxtaposition of songs that were like the soundtrack to a surrealistic film preceding a sublime and timeless lullaby. 'The White Album' represented the synthesis of all that the Beatles had learned about studio technique–applied over four months of arduous working, reworking and fine tuning, with the talent of George Martin and all the technical resources of EMI at their disposal every step of the way. They were a stunning five months of sessions, with hours of some of the most complex sessions ever recorded. Whereas most of the early Beatles songs were recorded in two or three takes, and the *Revolver* songs in up to 20, many of the 'The White Album' tracks went through as many as 196 permutations before their exacting creators were satisfied. Indeed, their final session for the album lasted *24 hours*, from 5 pm on 16 October to 5 pm the following day!

In the opening piece, Paul McCartney framed a rock-and-roll classic as a combination image of Ray Charles' *Georgia On My*

Mind and Chuck Berry's *Back in the USA*, which he set in the Soviet Union. McCartney took stock-in-trade rock and roll themes that had served everyone from Buddy Holly to Brian Wilson, recast them with a Soviet backdrop, and called it (what else?) *Back in the USSR*. 'Well the Ukraine girls really knock me out,' he wrote, 'they leave the West behind; and Moscow girls make me sing and shout, and Georgia's always on my mind.' Tongue in cheek, he added: 'Show me 'round your snow-peaked mountains way down south. Take me to your daddy's farm. Let me hear your balalaikas ringing out, come and keep your comrade warm.'

'The White Album' certainly included many of the best songs that any of the Beatles ever wrote. Ringo Starr, for instance, composed only two songs in his entire Beatles career (and very few since), and *Don't Pass Me By* from 'The White Album' has to be the most enduring one.

George Harrison's *While My Guitar Gently Weeps* (recorded here with Eric Clapton on lead) is recognized as perhaps his greatest—and certainly his most definitive—work, while *Long, Long, Long* is one of the best love songs of all time.

Paul McCartney was in rare form when he turned *Martha My Dear*, a song he'd written for his sheep dog, into a classic love song. His *Blackbird* is both musically and lyrically equal to *Yesterday* or *Michelle* as a pop standard. 'Blackbird singing in the dead of night,' he wrote, 'Take these broken wings and learn to fly. All your life... You were only waiting for this moment to arise. Blackbird singing in the dead of night, take these sunken eyes and learn to see... All your life... You were only waiting for

this moment to be free.' How can one fault such lyrics? Nor did he miss the mark with *Rocky Raccoon*, another double-pronged parody, this time an English music hall ballad with the words and melody of a cowboy song, which he had recorded on 15 August with only George Martin on piano as accompaniment.

John Lennon also produced several of his best works for this album. Even Bob Dylan at his peak would have been hard-pressed to equal Lennon's imagery in *Happiness Is a Warm Gun*: 'She's not a girl who misses much. She's well acquainted with the touch of the velvet hand, like a lizard on a window pane.'

Like McCartney, Lennon's work on this album was incredibly diverse. In *Yer Blues*, a worm licks the bones of a man so lonely he wants to die. This vicious pessimism is in stark contrast to *Julia*, which was written for his mother who had died 10 years earlier in an automobile accident. It is one of the gentlest and most beautiful songs of his repertoire. Striking off into yet another direction, Lennon's *Cry Baby Cry* is a strange surrealist children's story in the *I Am the Walrus* mold, populated by the King of Marigold, the Duchess of Kirkaldy and others who gather ''round the table for a seance in the dark, with voices out of nowhere put on "specially by the children for a lark".'

Also included on 'The White Album' are two of as many as 22 different versions of *Revolution*. Side four of the album begins with a song designated as *Revolution 1*. It was, in fact, a slower version of *Revolution* which had appeared three months earlier on the flip side of *Hey Jude* (which has been provisionally identified as *Revolution 2*). *Revolution 9*, on the other hand, was a horse of a very different color, and is completely different. Unlike the other two publicly known *Revolutions*, it is a 10-minute audio collage inspired by Paul McCartney's fascination with avante garde composer Karlheinz Stockhausen. Similar to their *Carnival of Light* soundtrack, *Revolution 9*, created by McCartney and Lennon using tape loops of sounds, voices and Beatlemania screams played backward, over which a narrator repeats the mantra, 'Number nine, number nine...' The other six or eight *Revolutions* remain officially unreleased. It is uncertain how many of the 22 or more studio and rehearsal takes represent simply repetitions of virtually identical takes, and how many are actually variations that are as different from one another as are *Revolutions 1, 2* and *9*. Several of them, including those designated as *Revolution 4* and *Revolution 5*, have been in circulation among collectors for many years. *Revolution 18*, recorded on 30 May 1968, was considered at the time to have been the most stunning and powerful of the sessions. Only its 10-minute length kept it from being the single, and alas, this also precluded it from album release.

During the first week of December, *The Beatles/*'The White Album' reached number one on the *Melody Maker* charts, and was certified as a gold record (250,000 units shipped) in the United States. The response to the album was the most enthusiastic that the group had received for any project since *Sgt Pepper*, and was certainly an improvement over the *Magical Mystery Tour* debacle of a year earlier.

The Beatles appeared to have regained the Midas touch. After three years of Beatlemania, they had retired to a studio in 1966. Yet in 1967, and now again in 1968, they had amazed the world and pleased their legions of fans with milestone masterworks. It was as though they could do no wrong. The optimism born of the success of the release of 'The White Album' and the publicity that accompanied the simultaneous nationwide American release of the *Yellow Submarine* film, lifted their spirits to heights untouched since before Brian Epstein's death. As yet another unbelievable year wound down, there was renewed talk of the Beatles once again becoming a road show.

1 9 6 9

HELLO. GOODBYE.

'Pick up the banjo and get in the limousine. Soon we'll be away from here. Step on the gas and wipe that tear away. One sweet dream came true today…came true today.'
–*John Lennon and Paul McCartney (1969)*

The momentum generated by *Yellow Submarine* and 'The White Album' swept the Beatles and Apple Corps into the new year on a wave of enthusiasm for new projects. The *Yellow Submarine* soundtrack album, recorded nearly a year earlier, was released in both the United Kingdom and the United States in mid-January. It was the fifth album for Apple. James Taylor's first Apple album had been released the previous month, and *Postcard*, the first album by Mary Hopkin, was nearing completion. George Harrison had completed an electronic album and was collaborating with Derek Taylor on a stage play based on Apple Corps office politics.

On 2 January the Beatles began work on what was to have been the most grandiose, multimedia project of their career, something to make *Magical Mystery Tour* seem like a weekend in the country. As originally conceived, a documentary film would be made of the Beatles recording an album. This process was alternately discussed in the context of a television special, or in a situation whereby both the album and film would be released publicly in conjunction with either a concert tour or a single, large concert, which would itself be broadcast, filmed and recorded. However, even as the first recording session got under way at the massive Twickenham film studios in London, things disintegrated as members of the group began to argue among themselves. By 10 January the idea of a live show was shelved when George Harrison decided he did not want to participate.

Despite general disagreement about the ultimate outcome of the project, the group members continued to rehearse and record, as the cameras rolled, at both Twickenham and at a new recording studio that they had installed at Apple Corps headquarters on Savile Row. During these sessions, the Beatles recorded over 100 songs, but, unlike the smaller number of *original* works which came out of 'The White Album' sessions six months earlier, most were rock-and-roll standards written by others.

Another notable difference between this session and that of summer 1968 was the fact that 28 hours of it was filmed for posterity. As the sessions proceeded, about one dozen Lennon, McCartney and Harrison songs were brought to completion, and two of these, *Get Back* and *Don't Let Me Down*, were chosen for

Top: **George Harrison in a lighter moment during the January 1969 sessions.** *Above:* **Lennon at Twickenham with the omnipresent Ono just over his shoulder.** *Facing page:* **John, Paul and Ringo in cold and cavernous Twickenham as the cameras roll.**

later release as a single. Indeed, the notion of 'Getting Back' evolved as the theme of these sessions, wherein the Beatles got back to the simpler sound of their rock-and-roll roots, the simpler sound of the classics that dominated so much of their repertoire when they first started out together.

The climax of these 'Get Back' sessions came on 30 January, when they moved their equipment to the top of the Apple Corps building for what would be their last public concert ever. With Apple recording artist Billy Preston–an old friend from their Hamburg days–backing them on keyboards, they played several versions of four Lennon-McCartney songs from their current sessions: *I've Got a Feeling*, *One After 909*, *I Dig a Pony*, and *Get Back*.

The audience for the 42-minute 'concert' was comprised of Apple staff members, who had gone up to join them on the rooftop, and people in the adjacent office buildings, who were able to crane their necks to see. The music could be heard clearly in the surrounding blocks and on busy Regent Street, one street behind them. On the streets below, traffic came to a standstill and the police were called to halt the concert. A month of filming ended the day after this rooftop concert, but the Beatles continued to work on the Lennon, McCartney and Harrison songs they'd started, polishing them for an eventual album.

The principal focus of Apple Corps had, by now, moved to the business offices. Lack of management, which had plagued the company since its inception a year earlier, finally took its toll. In the beginning, it hadn't seemed to matter. The Beatles had so much money that it seemed like Apple could do almost anything. Appearances, however, can be deceiving, and by January 1969 it was obvious that the previous year's problem with the

Above left: **Paul McCartney strums a guitar solo as a bored Ringo looks on from behind his drum baffle.** *Above:* **George Harrison looking chipper in his velvet bow tie, a light moment in the 'Get Back' sessions, which were characterized more by the mood expressed by Lennon on the** *facing page.*

Apple Boutique, which had *seemed* like an isolated instance, was actually symptomatic of what was happening throughout the entire Apple empire. Quite simply, the company was losing money faster than even the Beatles could earn it back. John Lennon even went so far as to say that the Beatles/Apple Corps partnership would soon be broke.

The evolution of the *Get Back* album, *Get Back* film and, indeed, the whole *Get Back* multimedia project, was a good example of how Apple itself, as a doomed company, began to unravel in the spring of 1969. The tracks for the *Get Back* album were completed by the Beatles in February, and George Martin finished most of his production work in March. The final remix of the title track came on 7 April and *Get Back* b/w *Don't Let Me Down* were released as a single in England on 11 April, and in the United States three days later. Also scheduled for release in April, the *Get Back* album had its debut postponed to August. When it *was* released, however, it was released to only a handful of radio stations and then it was promptly recalled. By year's end, the *Get Back* single was the only artifact in circulation from what was to have been the Beatles' grandest project ever.

It was against this backdrop that a new cast of characters entered to pick over the mess that Apple had become. On one hand was Clive Epstein, brother of the Beatles' late manager and owner of Brian Epstein's NEMS holding company (now much more vast than simply the original North England Music Stores). Next, there was American record company executive

Allen Klein, who John Lennon proposed be hired as financial manager of Apple. Finally, there was the New York law firm of (John) Eastman & (Lee) Eastman, the father and brother of Linda Eastman, Paul McCartney's girlfriend and soon-to-be wife. Allen Klein was officially appointed as the business manager for all the Beatles on 3 February, and Eastman & Eastman became the group's legal counsel the following day.

The rift that was to develop between Klein and the Eastmans paralleled the developing feud between Lennon and McCartney. Both John and George desperately yearned for a hard-nosed businessman to step in and straighten out the unraveling Apple empire, and Allen Klein was the archetype. Paul naturally gravitated toward his in-laws. The two sides of the rift could not have been more contrasting. Klein was a street fighter, an accountant whose credentials reflected years of wheeling and dealing on Broadway and 'tin pan alley,' and whose management credits included the Rolling Stones. The Eastmans were strictly Ivy League, with Lee a Harvard alumni and John a graduate of Stanford and the NYU law school.

With Paul McCartney's blessing, the Eastmans began by offering Clive Epstein one million pounds for NEMS, with the money to be borrowed from EMI against future royalties. John Lennon, however, insisted that he would deal only with Klein, who didn't want to go ahead with a NEMS buy out until the actual net worth of the Beatles and Apple could be ascertained. Estimates varied by as much as one million pounds. Much to the chagrin of all concerned, the deal fell through, and in February 1969 Clive sold NEMS to the Triumph Investment Trust, which was headed by corporate raider Leonard Richtenberg.

Stunned by this turn of events, all four Beatles jointly requested that EMI pay all their future royalties to Apple rather than NEMS. Timing was critical because a royalty for about £1.3 million was coming due on 31 March. A great deal of hard bargaining ensued, in which Richtenberg essentially *sold* to the Beatles the rights that NEMS had to their royalties. Paul McCartney differed with the others on whether to accept the deal, which had been arranged by Allen Klein, and the wedge between him and John Lennon was driven a little deeper.

In his new-found role as business manager for the Beatles and Apple, Klein's brash New York style won him few friends in the laid-back atmosphere of the Apple offices on Savile Row. The January rooftop concert was to be the last of the great Apple office parties. Klein cut through the fabric of the place like a buzz saw through balsa. He saw waste and inefficiency and dealt

Upper left: **The Beatles, bundled against the cold, along with Billy Preston** *(top center, beside organ)* **on the Apple Corps roof for their last public concert on 30 January 1969. Only Apple staffers and workers in nearby office buildings witnessed the concert.** *Above:* **Downstairs in the Apple studio, John Lennon ponders a chord while George Harrison** *(above right)* **locates a missing microphone jack.** *Below:*

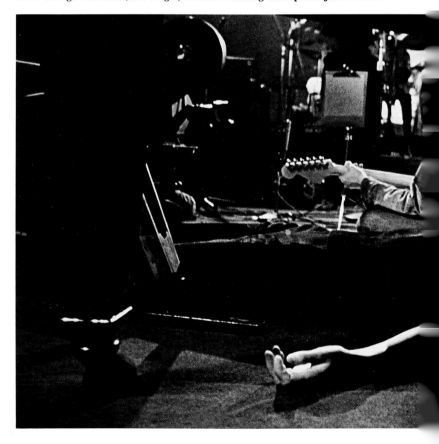

Yoko Ono snoozes under McCartney's grand piano while Lennon and Harrison trade guitar licks during a midnight session for the *Get Back* album. *Far right:* Surrounded by the Beatles, a glum George Martin watches Yoko Ono preside over the control board as he ponders the imminent end of the sparkling creative force that he has known for five magic years.

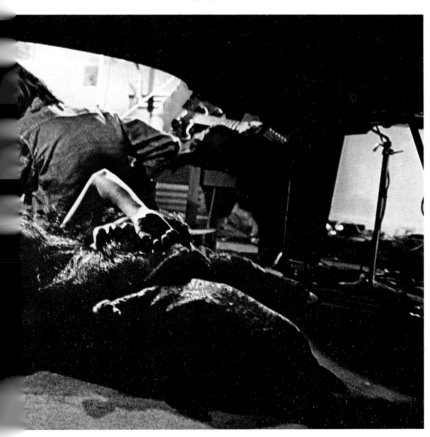

with it the only way he knew how. To his credit, however, he was firing many people that Brian Epstein never would have hired and eliminating jobs that Brian Epstein never would have allowed to be created. For 18 months, Apple itself had been a 'magical mystery tour.' No more.

Apple Corps itself, despite the efforts of Allen Klein and the Eastmans to prop it up, began to succumb to the Beatles' lack of attention. The grandiose effort at building a catalog of diverse artists, that had begun with such fanfare a year before, began to falter. Any artists that weren't aboard by March 1969 never had a chance with Apple. Mary Hopkin and Jackie Lomax remained, but the Modern Jazz Quartet and James Taylor left to find greater stardom elsewhere. Produced by George Harrison, Billy Preston's album *That's the Way God Planned It*, released at the end of August, did well, and the Iveys (later to become Badfinger) began a four year career on Apple.

Other than these few artists, however, Apple Records was on its way to changing from a potentially vibrant new label into a venue solely for the Beatles, their friends and various eccentric projects—such as George Harrison's recordings of the Radha Krishna Temple and the experimental, extemporaneous projects that John Lennon was working on with Yoko Ono.

On 11 March Paul and Linda Eastman announced that they would be married the following day. The decision being made in some haste, Paul had to convince a jeweler that evening to open his shop after hours in order to buy a wedding ring. The wedding took place on 12 March at the Marylebone Register Office in London, with Paul's brother Mike as best man. Four days later the McCartneys left for New York to visit Linda's family, even as John Lennon and Yoko Ono were traveling to France, where they intended to wed in Paris.

Ultimately, however, John and Yoko were married on 20 March during a quickly arranged half-day visit to Gibraltar, after which they flew to Amsterdam. Ensconced at the Amsterdam Hilton, they turned their honeymoon into a 'Bed-In' for peace—actually a week-long press conference held in their hotel room, during which they spoke to the press while reclining on their king-size bed.

Having achieved an extraordinary amount of coverage from the world press for their 'Bed-In,' John and Yoko turned their lives into a multimedia road show based on an ambiguous theme of promoting world peace. While in retrospect it is hard to see how anything they did actually promoted world peace, it is certain that they were successfully able to promote their own status as avant garde media celebrities. Dressed entirely in white, they darted off to Vienna at the end of March to premier their experimental film *Rape*.

John chronicled this entire odyssey in the song *The Ballad of John and Yoko*, which the Beatles recorded on 22 April. It was released five weeks later with George Harrison's *Old Brown Shoe* on the flip side. In *The Ballad of John and Yoko* Lennon complained about the press treatment that had, ironically, helped sell Beatles products despite underscoring his own eccentricity. Of the 'Bed-In,' he wrote: 'Drove from Paris to the Amsterdam Hilton, talking in our bed for a week. The newspapers said, say what're you doing in bed, I said we're only trying to get us some peace.'

His commentary on their Vienna soiree underscored the media's view of their relationship, which was not so much negative as one not to be taken as seriously as John would have liked: 'Made a lightning trip to Vienna, eating choc'late cake in a bag,' he wrote. 'The newspapers said, she's' gone to his head, they look just like two Gurus in drag. Christ! You know it ain't easy, you know how hard it can be. The way things are going, they're going to crucify me.'

The reference to the 'bag' alluded to their unusual practice in Vienna of conducting press conferences from inside a large bag. Although this activity was eventually abandoned, the couple adopted the name for their own informal umbrella company, Bag Productions, which they formed on 24 May to publish records. It was an exuberant scheme of inconspicuous outcome.

The *Ballad of John and Yoko* easily could have continued its lyric story with John changing his middle name–from Winston to Ono–on the roof of the Apple building on the same day that the song was recorded. The *Ballad of John and Yoko* actually would be the *last* song that the Beatles would record specifically for release as a single, but by no means was it the only single that John recorded during 1969. Indeed, this year was the most prolific ever for his independent recording career, which had been launched six months before with the debut of *Two Virgins*.

On 9 May, John and Yoko released their second documentary album, a sequel of sorts to *Two Virgins*, which was entitled *Unfinished Music 2: Life With the Lions*. Side two had been recorded in Queen Charlotte Hospital in November 1968 immediately prior to Yoko's miscarriage, while side one had been recorded at an avant garde musical performance they had given at Lady Mitchell Hall in Cambridge on 2 March 1969. The album was released on Apple's 'spoken word specialty' label, 'Zapple,' with the serial number '01.'

Released in the United States on 26 May, the album also was identified as a 'Zapple' album, but it carried a Capitol records serial number. Although Capitol had refused to distribute their earlier album due to its risqué cover photo, apparently even the presence of one track on the *Life With the Lions* album, entitled *Two Minutes of Silence* (which was exactly that), failed to put them off the chance at a Beatles-related product.

A second album on Apple's short-lived 'Zapple' subsidiary, released on the same dates as *Life With the Lions*, was George Harrison's *Electronic Sound*, also recorded between November and March. Like the John and Yoko album, it carried a 'Zapple' serial (02) in the United Kingdom and a Capitol serial number in the United States.

John and Yoko's plan to take their 'magical mystery tour' to the United States was derailed when John was denied an American visa because of a minor drug arrest in England. As an alternative, they flew to Montreal, Quebec, taking with them Yoko's six-year-old daughter, Kyoko Cox. There they staged a second 10-day 'Bed-In' in Room 1742 of the Queen Elizabeth Hotel, which coincided with the release of *Life With the Lions* in the United States. It was also during the Montreal 'Bed-In' that *The Ballad of John and Yoko* was released.

On 1 June, still under the sheets in the midst of their 'Bed-In,' they recorded–along with a chorus of onlookers–their first single, *Give Peace a Chance*, which was written by John (although credited to Lennon-McCartney for legal reasons) and was backed with Yoko's *Remember Love*. Released worldwide a month later, the single was credited as having been recorded by the 'Plastic Ono Band,' the name John would assign to designate the many bands that he would perform or record with in the upcoming years. This name was used regardless of the specific personnel in the band, as John, and occasionally Yoko, were its only permanent 'members.' *Give Peace a Chance*, which sounded very much like a sequel to *The Ballad of John and Yoko*, went on to become almost a theme song for Lennon in his post-Beatles career.

The on-stage debut of the Plastic Ono Band quickly followed as the result of a decision that John spontaneously made on 12 September. He had received a phone call from John Brower and Ken Walker, producers of the Toronto Rock And Roll Revival, a rock festival scheduled for the following day at the city's Varsity Stadium. Lennon said he'd play if he was able to get a band together. It would be the Plastic Ono band, and not the famous foursome.

Through George Harrison he was able to contact Eric Clapton, one of history's most prominent rock guitarists, who at that time was the reigning king of the lead guitar. Clapton's credits included a several-year stint with the rock band Cream, and a recent road tour with Blind Faith, the first band ever to have been described as a 'supergroup' (a term that was coined to describe a group composed of the key musicians from several major groups, brought together to form one, 'super,' group). Clapton also had previously worked with the Beatles themselves on 'The White Album' sessions. With Clapton on his team, Lennon lined up the rest of the band, which included *Revolver* cover artist (and an old friend from his Hamburg days), Klaus Voorman, on bass.

Arriving on stage just after Jerry Lee Lewis and Chuck Berry had finished their sets, Lennon nervously addressed an audience

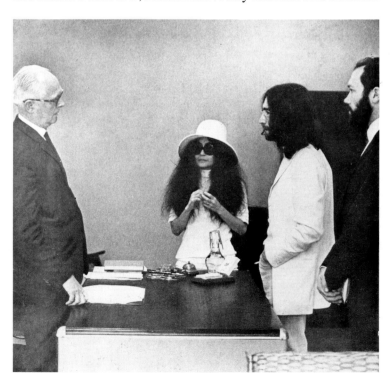

of 20,000, who gave him a tumultuous welcome. 'We're only going to play numbers we know,' he told his first audience in over three years, 'cause we never played together before…'

The crowd didn't seem to mind, and the Plastic Ono Band performed Carl Perkins' *Blue Suede Shoes* and several other

Life with the Lennons *(above)* in 1969 was a frantic slapstick of lie-ins, love-ins, and conceptual art that took them from Amsterdam to Vienna to Toronto. Square one had been a dash to Gibraltar for a quick wedding *(below)* on 20 March. 'We're going to stage many happenings together, and the wedding was one of them,' Yoko remarked to the press. They would.

rock-and-roll classics before doing John's *Yer Blues* from 'The White Album.' This was followed by *Cold Turkey* (a new song in the pessimistic *Yer Blues* mood) and *Give Peace a Chance*, which turned into an audience singalong.

Yoko Ono joined the band for *Don't Worry Kyoko (Mummy's Only Looking for Her Hand in The Snow)* and *John John (Let's Hope for Peace)*, two songs whose avant garde nature was compared in *Rolling Stone* magazine to 'the *cri du coeur* of a woman in intense anxiety.' The concert was recorded and was subsequently released on 12 December as the *Live Peace in Toronto 1969* album, which was, remarkably, the first live album featuring any member of the Beatles that had ever been released.

In the wake of the concert's success, John considered taking the new band on the road, but other projects intervened and his interest was dissipated. John and Yoko went on to record *Cold Turkey* b/w *Don't Cry Kyoko* on 30 September, for release as a single three weeks later. They also put the finishing touches on *The Wedding Album*, which was released on 20 October in the United States and on 7 November in England.

The Wedding Album was packaged in a 12-inch box containing artifacts from their wedding in Gibraltar and honeymoon in Amsterdam, including a full-color facsimile of their marriage license, photos of the wedding, a booklet of press clippings and a full-size close-up photo of a piece of wedding cake. The single disc LP was largely composed of dialogue and ambient noise recorded during March and April 1969 in London (side one) and during the Amsterdam 'Bed-In' (side two). *The Wedding Album* proved to be an interesting collector's item–certainly a must for every die-hard John and Yoko fan–but its high price and esoteric nature gave it only a three-week tenure on the *Billboard* album charts, where it fluctuated between 178 and 182.

Even as John was garnering headlines with his antics with Yoko, the Beatles continued to record. The *Get Back* album was completed and in the can, pending its April release (that would never materialize), when the Beatles set to work on their second major recording effort of the year. This time the theme was more in line with the complexity of *Sgt Pepper* and 'The White Album' than it was with the simplicity of the *Get Back* sessions. This also meant they had to use EMI's Abbey Road studios rather than the newer, but less complete, Apple studios on Savile Row.

By the end of August, over 30 songs (a few of which dated back to January) had been recorded for the new album, of which 17 would ultimately be incorporated into an album, including the components of a six-song jam on side two. *The Ballad of John and Yoko* was recorded concurrently, but was intended only as a single release, while *Old Brown Shoe*, one of the earliest songs from these album sessions, was chosen as the B side and was not reused on the album.

Originally, the album was to be named *Everest*, after the brand of cigarettes favored by engineer Geoff Emerick. Elaborate plans were made to shoot the photograph for the jacket in the Himalayas, but ultimately the decision was made to simply name the album *Abbey Road*, for the studio where it was being taped. It would be the last one the Beatles would ever record together. At 10 o'clock on the morning of on 8 August, the Beatles went out into a crosswalk near the intersection of Abbey and Grove End Roads to be photographed by Iain MacMillan for the album jacket.

On 26 September, even as *Get Back* languished on the Apple Corps shelf, *Abbey Road* was released in England. After its release on 1 October in the United States, *Abbey Road* began an 87-week ride on the *Billboard* charts and was hailed as another masterpiece. Side one opened with John Lennon's *Come*

Together. This song was a brilliant satire crafted in the vein of *I Am the Walrus*, *Sexy Sadie* or *Happiness Is a Warm Gun*–in marked contrast to the then-recent ragged spontaneity of *Give Peace a Chance*. *Come Together* featured a raft of typically bizarre Lennon one-liners, such as 'hold you in his armchair, you can feel his disease,' and 'Got to be good looking 'cause he's so hard to see.'

For George Harrison, *Abbey Road* was, like 'The White Album' a year before, one of his best. *Something* and *Here Comes The Sun* would certainly rate a prominent role in any Harrison retrospective, even after a solo career nearly four times

as long as his Beatles career. Indeed, *Something* was released as the A side of the single from *Abbey Road*.

Paul McCartney also made a very good showing on the album. *Maxwell's Silver Hammer* was premier storytelling, while *Oh! Darling* was a delightfully camp waltz. Ringo Starr contributed the second of only two songs he wrote for a Beatles album, *Octopus's Garden*, one which would become something of a theme song for him in later years. Had he written it at a more auspicious time in the history of the Beatles, it may well have become the basis for another animated film like *Yellow Submarine*.

Despite the fact that the Beatles were caught up in a swirl of rumors of their imminent break-up, the six-song medley that closed the second side of *Abbey Road* made them appear more unified than they had in the past two years. *Mean Mr Mustard/Polythene Pam/She Came in through the Bathroom*

Below: **The most famous pedestrian crossing in London as it appeared to Iain MacMillan at 10:00 am on 8 August 1969. He snapped six pictures, and Paul McCartney picked one (of the four in which he had removed his shoes) for the album cover.** *Facing page:* **A contemplative John Lennon and family man Paul McCartney–very much alive–with stepdaughter Heather, who turned seven in 1969.**

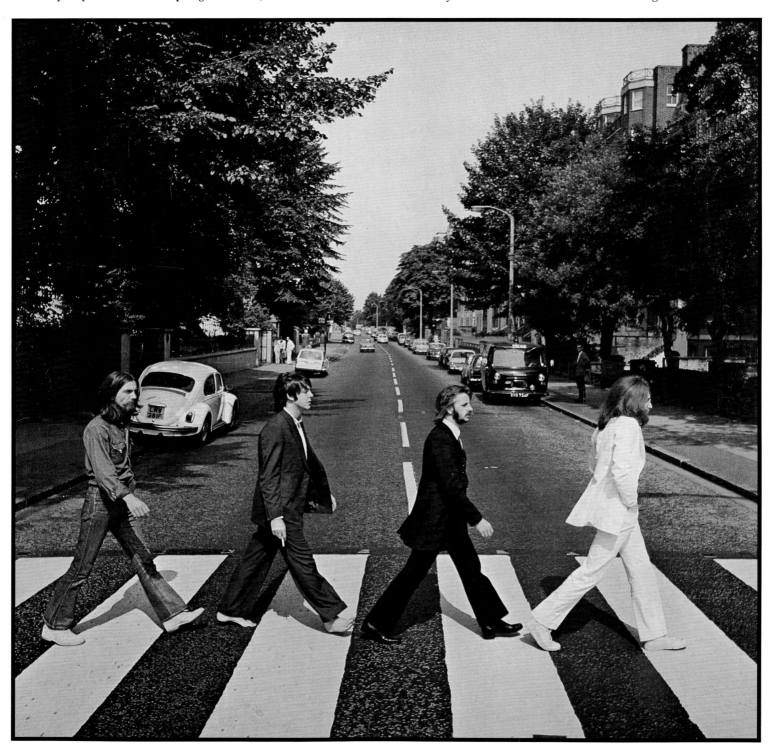

Window/Golden Slumbers/Carry That Weight/The End offered a breathtaking smorgasbord of lyrics and musical style that could arouse the kind of excitement rarely found outside a live concert. The album seemed to promise a bright future, but in fact, the end was close at hand. 'The White Album' ended with *Good Night* and *Abbey Road* closed with *The End*–so, perhaps we should have known. Paul McCartney tacked on his 23-second tribute to Queen Elizabeth II and that was it–the conclusion of the Beatles' last album.

By the time *Abbey Road* arrived in the shops, the Beatles had already gone their separate ways. The last time they would ever be in the same studio together had been on 20 August during the final remix. John, George and Ringo went to attend to various projects, both public and private, and Paul McCartney went to his farm in Scotland with his stepdaughter Heather, wife Linda and their new baby, Mary (who had been born on 28 August and was named for his mother). Even as Paul went into seclusion, rumors began to circulate that he was actually *dead*–killed in a 9 November 1966 car crash–and had been replaced by a double named William Campbell. The 'news' of Paul's death made headlines despite his efforts to quell the stories. The fact that he was barefoot on the *Abbey Road* cover photograph was taken as only one of many 'clues' to his death that appear on the various Beatles albums.

With Paul 'dead,' or at least in seclusion with his family, the idea of the Beatles going on tour again, or even playing a major, live, televised one-night stand, which had seemed like a real possibility at the beginning of the year, now appeared totally impossible. By the end of 1969, the Beatles had, as a group, turned down offers of one million dollars for a single concert, and $8.8 million for a 12-city American tour. But this wasn't a negative reaction to the idea of playing concerts so much as it was a recognition of the fact that the Beatles had, for all practical purposes, ceased to exist as an entity.

This did not mean, however, that the four individuals who made up the group did not have a yen for concert performances. Even though each of them had been quite emphatic–at various points during the year–about not performing in any more concerts as a foursome, at least two of them were actively playing concert dates with other groups. Without making a prior announcement, George Harrison–along with Eric Clapton and others–joined a tour of England and Denmark that had been packaged by Delaney and Bonnie Bramlett in early December.

Harrison played eight shows with Delaney and Bonnie, and then, on 15 December, joined John and Yoko for a benefit concert for UNICEF at London's Lyceum Gallery. The next day, John flew back to Toronto and announced that he would produce, and perform in, a three-day show to be held in Toronto in July 1970, to be called the Mosport Park Peace Festival. Though the festival plans would ultimately collapse, Lennon was so enthusiastic about the project at the time that he even met with Prime Minister Trudeau to discuss it in Ottawa on 22 December.

On the business side, meanwhile, things had not gone particularly well for the Beatles during 1969, even though the Eastmans and Allen Klein had succeeded in securing their record royalty rights from NEMS, and had cajoled EMI into increasing those royalties from 17.5 to 25 percent. However, Klein had failed to defeat a hostile takeover of Northern Songs, the Beatles' song publishing company, by Sir Lew Grade of Associated Television (ATV). This defeat was a bitter one for all four of the Beatles–and was even more so for the relations between John and Paul. Even their *victories* had been won at great emotional cost.

Though 1969 began as the year in which the Beatles would 'get back,' they didn't. They arranged for the elaborate filming of themselves recording an album, with the net result of only a single–no film and no album. They bickered, disagreed, appeared to break up and then, smoothly and effortlessly, recorded one of the most coherent albums of their career, even as the previous album gathered dust.

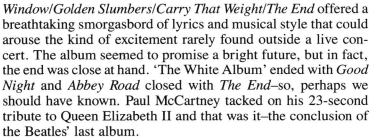

ALL THINGS MUST PASS

'All things must pass... All things must pass away.'

–*George Harrison (1970)*

It is difficult to specify the exact date when 'the Beatles' began, and it is equally hard to name the date when that extraordinary entity ceased to exist. During 1969 they had spent much more time apart than they had together, yet they had produced *Abbey Road*. They all had announced that they would never play concerts again, but both John and George *had*. What we do know for sure is that the last Beatles recording session (featuring the final takes of *I Me Mine*) took place on 3 January 1970 (John Lennon, however, was absent), and that, by the end of the year, the time had *passed* when all four would ever again stand together in the same room.

The year began with persistent rumors that the Beatles would soon part, or had already parted, company. Yet, it has been said that they had just begun work on a new album–one which they never would finish. Over 60 songs, including *Peace of Mind*, were allegedly recorded, yet only one–*I Me Mine*–was ever released.

There *were* Beatles albums released in 1970, but the only *new* material was on solo albums released by each of the group members. In February Capitol released an album called *The Beatles Again*, whose title seemed to imply that the material on the album was new, but it wasn't. It was merely a collection of hit singles dating from 1964-1969 that had never before appeared on a Capital album. The album was retitled *Hey Jude* shortly after its release to capitalize on the continuing popularity of the 1968 song.

In March Ringo Starr released his first album, called *Sentimental Journey*, which featured primarily vintage standards that he'd sung with his family as a child in the 1940s. Paul McCartney's inaugural solo album was the first mainstream rock album to be released individually by any of the Beatles and, as such, was seen by many people–notably John Lennon–as an effort to *compete* with the long-planned release of the Beatles' *Get Back* album.

Lennon's negative reaction proved to be yet another step in the gradually escalating feud between the two men that would mark the Beatles' demise. The album, called simply *McCartney*, had been recorded between November 1969 and March 1970. It entered record shops in the United Kingdom on 17 April and in the United States three days later. It was a true 'solo' album in the sense that Paul himself not only sang all the songs but, by using multiple recording tracks, he also played all the instruments as well!

Even as *McCartney* was released, the *Get Back* tapes continued to languish on the shelf, still awaiting release 14 months after they had been recorded. Because of this time lag–which was well known to fans–the freshness and spontaneity, that was originally present when the Beatles 'got back' to the simplicity of their pre-*Rubber Soul* roots, was somewhat lessened. For this reason, Allen Klein asked veteran Hollywood record producer Phil Spector to sift through the many hours of tapes and assemble a powerful album that would truly pay homage to the Beatles' image. Klein–as well as most of the Beatles–now felt uncomfortable with the light touch of George Martin's production on the *Get Back* tapes, and chose Spector because of his reputation for a lavish, multitracked 'wall of sound' production style. George Martin was himself dissatisfied with the *Get Back* sound because of the severe technical porblems encountered with the then-new recording equipment in the Apple recording studio at Savile Row. Indeed, Glyn Johns had done most of the hands-on production work.

In the meantime, 96 hours of *Get Back* film was being edited down to a marketable 88 minutes, and May 1970 was chosen for the movie's premier. In order to distance the 1970 album and film from those that were promised, yet not delivered, in 1969, it was

Facing page: **The Beatles from their last photo opportunity. John Lennon and Yoko flew to Denmark to have their heads shaved on 20 January 1970, and everyone went their separate ways.**

decided to *rename* the project, thereby giving it the *appearance* of being a *new* project. Thus, the *Get Back* multimedia event became the *Let It Be* film and accompanying soundtrack album. The title song, recorded during the *Get Back* sessions, was 'reproduced' by Phil Spector and was released as a single on 6 March in the United Kingdom and five days later in America. The B side to the *Let It Be* single, *You Know My Name (Look Up My Number)*, was chosen from among the outtakes from the 1967 *Sgt Pepper* sessions, perhaps to infuse the 'new' project with some of the magic of *Sgt Pepper*.

On 8 May, two months after the single was released, the entire *Let It Be* album, as 'reproduced' by Phil Spector–including versions of *Get Back* and *Don't Let Me Down*–was released in the United Kingdom. Spector's work was clearly evident in the layers of background instrumentation that he had added. However, despite its being much more 'heavily produced' than the

George Martin/Glyn Johns *Get Back*, Spector's work in the *Let It Be* album was surprisingly understated and subtle when compared to the work he'd done in the mid-1960s, for which he'd earned a reputation for 'overproduction.'

Coming after an annual succession of five milestone albums–beginning with *Rubber Soul* in 1966 and ending with *Abbey Road* in 1969–*Let It Be* seemed like an anticlimax. True, there were moments of greatness on the album, but *Let It Be* was clearly overshadowed by the works that had preceded it.

The *Let It Be* album's package was also heavily 'produced.' In the spirit of the original intent of the *Get Back* project, it was released in a black box, with a 160-page, full-color book featur-

Below: **The Beatles' 'last' album, recorded in January 1969 and not released until May 1970.** *Facing page:* **George Harrison from his landmark** *All Things Must Pass*, **also released in 1970. The album showcased Harrison's long-overshadowed talent as a songwriter.**

ing photographs from the original January 1969 sessions–photos of the same scenes that would appear in the film. When the album came out in the United States 10 days later, however, it was sans box and sans book, making the United Kingdom edition of *Let It Be* an instant collector's item.

The *Let It Be* film itself premiered in New York on 13 May, and in London and Liverpool on 20 May. The reaction of the critics served almost as an allegory for the careers of the Beatles themselves. As a film, the critics saw it as lacking in direction or focal point, but as a documentary–which preserved what the *Hollywood Reporter* called 'a moment in time'–it was considered priceless. Beyond this, however, *Let It Be* was simply a *cinema verite* experience that had been conceived as part of a multi-media event that never happened; a film that was edited into a form never intended, long after the people who created the original material had lost interest in it. Like the album, *Let It Be* the movie, was anticlimatic.

For all practical purposes, the Beatles had ceased to exist by the time the *Let It Be* album and film were released. In early April Paul McCartney began to refer publicly to the Beatles in the past tense, and both John Lennon and George Harrison acknowledged that he'd left the group, although George described this situation as 'temporary.'

The Apple press office and the various Beatles fan clubs sought to deny that anything had happened, but in August Paul wrote to John asking that the Beatles partnership, the entity which evolved into Apple Corps, be dissolved. In November a tax authority writ was filed against the partnership by the British government. With the help of Eastman & Eastman–his in-laws and lawyers–Paul initiated legal proceedings to end his relationship with the group. This activity ultimately led to his filing suit against the partnership and, in effect, against John, George and Ringo individually. The suit was filed on 31 December 1970. The Beatles were no more.

Ironically, the breakup came more as a whimper than a bang. Like the *Let It Be* album and film, Paul McCartney's lawsuit was something of an anticlimax. The beginning of the end actually had come in April, when Paul McCartney announced that he was out. Then the Apple Press office had been closed in August. The group hadn't even made a pretense of recording together since January, and each of them had gone on to pursue individual projects. Ringo went to to Nashville at the end of June to record *Beaucoups of Blues* for September release, and George Harrison spent the summer on what *Rolling Stone* magazine would call 'the *War and Peace* of rock albums.'

Harrison's *All Things Must Pass* was a three-record set on which he was backed by some of the best musicians in the world–from Eric Clapton and Duane Allman on guitar, to Ringo Starr (the only ex-Beatle included) on drums. For years, Harrison the songwriter had been overshadowed by Lennon and McCartney. He had averaged only two songs per album with the Beatles, while John and Paul had each contributed five or six. *All Things Must Pass* represented the culmination of years of songwriting from the man who'd given *While My Guitar Gently Weeps* to the *White Album*, and *Something* to *Abbey Road*. *All Things Must Pass* was monumental for both its size and for its quality. It stands as George Harrison's best solo album and it can arguably be considered as the best individual–or group–Beatle album of 1970.

John Lennon had been a ubiquitous part of the limelight in 1969, ending the year in the headlines and featured prominently on the BBC's 'Man of the Decade' retrospective. In 1970 it was quite the opposite. In 1969 he'd released three solo albums and two solo singles. By December 1970 he had released only the

Plastic Ono Band single *Instant Karma*, which had been issued back in February. In the meantime, Paul McCartney had released an album; Ringo, two albums; and George Harrison a *magnum opus*. But Lennon's turn finally came on 11 December, with his first all-rock, nonexperimental solo album, which was entitled simply *Plastic Ono Band*. This album was accompanied by the simultaneous release of a solo album by Yoko Ono, *also* entitled *Plastic Ono Band*, which featured a virtually identical cover photo, but vastly dissimilar music.

John's album was a deeply personal and introspective work that was viewed by some as bordering on psychotic. It featured uncharacteristic songs about God and about his mother, and served to document the pain and suffering that he had experienced both in the wake of Yoko's second miscarriage in August 1970, and also in the course of his therapy with Hollywood pop psychologist Arthur Janov. John and Yoko had spent several months in California with Janov, author of the book *Primal Scream*, whose title summarized his idea of the key to well being. The emotions that first spilled out in Janov's padded rooms clearly made their way onto the tracks of *Plastic Ono Band*.

If George Harrison's 1970 album can be taken to embody the *end* of an era, then certainly John Lennon's 1970 album was the first milestone to mark a future without the Beatles. Lennon concluded *Plastic Ono Band* with the short track *My Mummy's Dead*, clearly a reference to Julia Lennon–who had been killed in 1958 –but it could also be seen as a metaphor for the death of the Beatles as a group. The Beatles had been his family since he was barely more than a teenager, as it had been for Paul, George and Ringo. They had all come to feel repressed and constrained by that family, but it had been an entity that had given them–and the world–so much for so long. And now it was gone. The four parts were no longer a whole, and each one of them now embarked on a new decade alone.

E P I L O G U E

ACROSS THE UNIVERSE

'Mama don't go…Daddy come home!'
–John Lennon (1970)

'Close your eyes, have no fear. The monster's gone, he's on the run and your daddy's here.'
–John Lennon (1980)

It was the night of Monday, 8 December 1980, and a cold winter wind was whipping through the streets of New York City as John Lennon and Yoko Ono returned home from a recording session at the Record Plant. Home was–and had been for several years–a 25-room apartment in the Dakota, a neogothic apartment building on Central Park West, which they shared with their five-year-old son, Sean. There, life had been one of semi-seclusion, until the release of their *Double Fantasy* album just three weeks earlier on 17 November. John hadn't released any new material in over five years and now, suddenly, the Lennons were in the limelight once again. Fans and critics alike had praised *Double Fantasy*, and there was a good deal of excitement about the new album that John already had in the works.

Against this backdrop, it is little wonder that occasional small groups of fans would haunt the Dakota's entrance to catch a glimpse of, or possibly get an autograph from, the famous couple. Among those gathered on this bitter winter evening was one Mark David Chapman, a Georgia-born ex-security guard, late of Hawaii, who had managed to garner an autograph from Lennon on this very sidewalk just a few hours before. Born the year that *Help*! had premiered, Chapman had grown up obsessed with the Beatles. Yet, there is no way to fathom why he came to do what he did that night. As John Lennon emerged from his car and began to follow Yoko Ono toward the entrance to the Dakota, Chapman crouched down, whipped a pistol from his pocket and began to fire. John took six steps and collapsed. The man who had helped to create one of the most renowned musical phenomena of all time died two weeks before Christmas, just two months into his 41st year.

Public reaction was much like that evoked by the assassinations of the Kennedy brothers, and Dr Martin Luther King, in the 1960s. It was front page news on television and in the newspapers. *Time* magazine did a cover story. Thousands of fans came to stand on the hills of Central Park–across the street from the Dakota–to mourn Lennon and sing his songs. But one of the most moving tributes to him came from the man who probably had made the biggest impact on Lennon's life, even though in later years they were separated by a feud: Said Paul McCartney, 'I can't tell you how much it hurts to lose him. His death is a bitter, cruel blow. I really loved the guy.'

The creative contributions made by Lennon and McCartney to the Beatles had been roughly equal, but there was something about Lennon's brilliantly eccentric style–both in his his personal and musical lives–that made him the embodiment of the what the Beatles had been and would always be. His death came exactly one decade after the Beatles disbanded, but it was the final blow. Throughout that decade, there always had been the hope that somehow the magic that had been the Beatles could someday live again. With Lennon's death, this clearly would never be.

The decade had begun with almost as many rumors of a Beatles reunion in 1971 as there had been of the Beatles' demise a year earlier. Between February and April 1971, each of the former Beatles had released a single, and Paul McCartney's second album, *Ram*, was released on 17 May.

In the meantime, on the other side of the world, completely

Facing page: **Yoko Ono and John Lennon in New York City shortly before Lennon's assassination in 1980.**

82

unrelated events were shaping up to form an event that *could* have led to a possible reunion. The ethnic Bengali majority of what was then East Pakistan was fighting for independence from predominantly Moslem West Pakistan, declaring themselves to be the independent 'Bangla Desh' (Bengal Nation). In the course of the fighting, one million Bengalis were killed and another *10 million* took refuge in the Indian province of West Bengal, which was predominantly populated by ethnic Bengalis. Millions of dollars were needed to help stave off death by starvation.

George Harrison's old friend, Ravi Shankar–himself an Indian citizen–appealed to George for help. The former Beatle initially recorded a song about the situation, appropriately titled *Bangla Desh*, which was released on 28 July 1971, with all proceeds from the record's sales earmarked for Bengali relief. Harrison's generosity served to draw attention to the problem, as well as raise money. In the meantime, George also conceived the idea of a concert to raise further funds. What resulted was an unprecedented program which became an archetype for all the superstar 'mega-concerts' that would follow in the years to come.

The two shows that were given on 1 August, at New York's Madison Square Garden, brought together a truly incredible line up of musicians. Each concert opened with a set by Ravi Shankar and his ensemble, followed by a full-fledged rock show, with Harrison backed by a host of prominent musicians, including Eric Clapton, Leon Russell, Billy Preston and Ringo Starr. The climax of the shows was Bob Dylan's appearance for five songs. Dylan sang and played acoustic guitar, while Ringo Starr played tambourine. Joining them were Leon Russell on bass guitar and George Harrison himself, who supplied the electric lead guitar.

The 'Concert for Bangla Desh' was the rock world's event of the year even though it did *not* result in the rumored reunion of the Beatles. Harrison had asked John and Paul (as well as Ringo) to join him, but Paul had refused because of their mutual, pending legal problems. John, who now lived in New York, had

initially agreed to the idea, but declined at the last moment. He was later said to have regretted this decision.

On 12 August 1971 Madison Square Garden counted up the gate receipts for the concert and cut a check for $248,418.50, payable to the United Nations Children's Fund for Relief to Refugee Children of Bangla Desh. On 20 December, a three-record live recording of the entire second show was released, with the intention of raising additional money. The concert was also filmed in 70mm by Twentieth Century Fox for theatrical release in March 1972.

In September 1971 John Lennon released his *Imagine* album, which would serve as a signature album for him for the rest of the decade. Its title track may well be the most memorable of his post-Beatles career. In fact, *Imagine* reappeared 17 years later as the title of an elaborate film about John's life that was produced in 1988 by David Wolper.

Over the next several years, John and Yoko became fixtures in the New York arts community. They took up residence on Bank Street in Greenwich Village, next door to the brownstone at number 105 in which John Cage, the great avant garde composer, made his home. Their album *Sometime in New York City*, which they released in June 1972, was almost like a scrapbook of their experiences, featuring songs about their social, as well as radical political, activities.

They were backed on it by a band called Elephant's Memory, which they had 'discovered' on one of their outings in New York. Included on the album was a collection of live material that was recorded during a surprise appearance that John had

A *New York Times* ad *(below right)* was the only public announcement of the 'Concert for Bangla Desh' but word of mouth made it a sell-out before the ad appeared. *Below, left to right:* Ringo Starr, George Harrison, Bob Dylan and Leon Russell on stage and a close-up of George Harrison *(above right)*. *Below far right:* The album recorded live at the 'Concert for Bangla Desh' was into the stores before Christmas, five and a half months later.

made with Frank Zappa's Mothers of Invention, at the Fillmore East on 6 June 1971. Also during this 1971-1973 'New York period,' John and Yoko produced a large number of avant garde home movies that were screened for the public at such respectable pantheons of the art world as the Whitney Museum and the Museum of Modern Art. These films also made it onto network television during John and Yoko's appearance on the Dick Cavett show in 1972.

It was an era of prolific output as well for Yoko Ono herself. During her earlier years in New York, where she had lived as a struggling artist before moving to London, no one had taken her seriously. In John, she had an avid patron and because of him, people *now* took her seriously. Between August 1971 and November 1972, Yoko recorded the material from which a pair of two-record sets were derived. *Fly* was released in September 1971 to coincide with John's *Imagine* album, and *Approximately Infinite Universe* followed in January 1973.

By early 1973, however, the first 'New York period' was coming to a close, and John's relationship with Yoko was foundering, due to his wanderlust. Shortly after moving uptown from Greenwich Village to their apartment at the Dakota, John became romantically involved with May Pang, a young Chinese-American woman whom the Lennons had hired as a valet/ secretary. At first, Yoko was indifferent to John's dalliance, rationalizing that it was better for John to have an affair with someone on *her* staff than an outsider. Soon, however, John was

spending more and more time in Los Angeles–frequently with May at his side–while Yoko remained behind in New York, sequestered in Apartment 72 at the Dakota.

John's artistic output during the year he spent commuting between New York and California was quite prolific and it soon gave rise to another round of Beatles reunion rumors. In March 1973, Ringo Starr had gone to the 'Golden State' to begin work on his third album, and he asked each of his three former colleagues to write a song for him. Not only did they write the songs, but they joined him in the recording studio as well. First, George Harrison wrote and recorded several songs with Ringo, then John Lennon contributed his *I'm the Greatest*, as well as background vocals. Finally, to everyone's surprise, Paul McCartney dropped in with his wife, Linda, to write and record *Six O'Clock*. With every member of the Beatles coming and going in the same studio during the same sessions for the first time in over three years, expectations that they would officially reunite flew about like confetti in the wind. In actuality, no more than three members of the old group were ever in the studio simultaneously, and Lennon and McCartney never came face to face.

Left: The cover for John Lennon's *Imagine*, released in 1971. *Right:* During this same period, John and Yoko's creative energies were also directed to filmmaking, and their films were shown at the Whitney Museum of Art. *Below, left to right:* Julian Lennon, Yoko Ono and Sean Lennon in 1985 at the premiere of Julian's home video *Stand by Me: A Portrait of Julian Lennon.*

When it was released in November 1973, the album *Ringo* marked the only time since 1970 that a single album of all-new material would feature all four Beatles, although none of the contributions of the four overlapped on any individual track.

Shortly after joining Ringo for his sessions, John Lennon recorded his third post-Beatles album, *Mind Games*, which was also released in November 1973. Also during this 1973-1974 'Los Angeles period,' Lennon began work on a collection of rock-and-roll oldies that eventually would be released in 1975. It was during this period of time, too, that he earned a reputation as a notable carouser. Estranged from his wife and occasionally accompanied by the 'younger woman,' John Lennon entered a two-year cycle of hard drinking, fast living, wild parties and adolescent antics. By September 1974, however, he had assembled enough material for his fourth album, *Walls and Bridges*.

As things turned out, this album would be his last for many years. Shortly after his reconcilement with Yoko in early 1975, she announced that she was pregnant and John began a half decade second 'New York period' in which he would be, as he later described himself, 'a househusband.' The oldies that he had recorded previously were released as an album entitled *Rock 'n' Roll* in February 1975, and in October 1975 Capitol and Parlophone released a John Lennon 'greatest hits' album called *Shaved Fish* for the Christmas season. Other than these two offerings, his second 'New York period' was spent in seclusion, a marked contrast to his 'Los Angeles period.'

Twice before, in 1968 and 1970, John and Yoko had been expecting a baby, and twice before Yoko had suffered a miscarriage. Having come through his 'adolescence' in Los Angeles, John was now ready to settle down and have a family. When his son Julian was born in 1963, John had not wanted anything to do with a family, and it was only in the mid-1970s that he finally

began to develop a relationship with his son. He now intended to make up for the deficiencies in that relationship by retiring to a 'househusbandom' status with his second-born child.

If nothing else, it always can be said that if John Lennon decided to do something, he always plunged into it with all the ferocity, zeal and commitment he could muster–which was usually considerable! This was no more evident than with Sean Ono Taro Lennon, born 9 October 1975, on his father's 35th birthday. It was not until the time of Sean's fifth birthday that his father returned to the recording studio to rekindle the fires of an earlier career, fires that burned brightly, but were destined to be snuffed out all too quickly.

After John's death in 1980, Yoko eventually completed the album they had been working on at the time he was killed, and it was finally released in 1984 under the name *Milk and Honey*. Meanwhile, a new generation was emerging–not only among the fans but among those musicians who were true inheritors of the Beatles' magic. Julian Lennon turned 21 in 1984 and released his own first album, *Valotte*. The single from the album, *Too Late for Goodbye*, which became a successful hit, was hauntingly reminiscent of his father's style. Julian's second album, *The Secret Value of Daydreaming* followed in 1986.

For Ringo Starr, 1973's *Ringo* was the high point of his post-Beatles recording career. His *Goodnight Vienna* (1974) was a moderate success, and was followed in 1975 by a Capitol/Parlophone 'Greatest Hits' album called *Blast from Your Past*. He subsequently recorded three albums for Polydor in 1976, 1977 and 1978 and one for RCA in 1981. By 1988, however, only *Ringo* and *Blast from Your Past* remain in release.

The *Ringo* cover art *(below left)* featured the cast of 'thousands' (including four Beatles) that helped to make it. *Below:* The diminutive John Lennon on the *Mind Games* cover was an allegorical flyspeck beneath the massive visage of Ono.

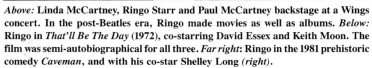

Above: Linda McCartney, Ringo Starr and Paul McCartney backstage at a Wings concert. In the post-Beatles era, Ringo made movies as well as albums. *Below:* Ringo in *That'll Be The Day* (1972), co-starring David Essex and Keith Moon. The film was semi-autobiographical for all three. *Far right:* Ringo in the 1981 prehistoric comedy *Caveman*, and with his co-star Shelley Long *(right)*.

Ringo's principal activities over these years centered more on acting than on recording. Even before the demise of the Beatles, he'd had a small role in the movie *Candy* (1967), and had starred, along with Peter Sellers, in *The Magic Christian* (1969). During the 1970s, he appeared *as* Frank Zappa in the latter's *200 Motels* (1971), and in the Italian Western *Blindman* (1971), as well as the pop horror film *Son of Dracula* (1974).

Ringo directed the film *Born to Boogie* in 1972 and appeared in another rock film, *That'll Be the Day*, in 1972. In 1975, along with Roger Daltry of The Who, he starred in *Lisztomania*, a film about the composer Franz Liszt (1811-1886). Daltry played the title role and Ringo played the pope! In 1977 he became involved in the production of the animated television feature *Scouse the Mouse*, and in 1987 he filmed a series of television commercials for Sun Country Wine Coolers, thereby becoming the first ex-Beatle to endorse a commercial product.

George Harrison had been responsible for two three-record albums (*All Things Must Pass* and *Concert for Bangla Desh*) in roughly a year's time, but his next record, *Living in the Material World* did not appear until the summer of 1973. His third post-Beatle rock album, *Dark Horse*, appeared in 1974, and the album *Extra Texture* was released to correspond with his 1975 North American tour.

The music world–the material world–that George Harrison toured in 1975 had changed considerably in the nine years since he had last toured with the Beatles. Even the metamorphosis wrought by the phenomenal late 1960s era had come and gone in the meantime. Jimi Hendrix and Janis Joplin had died in 1970

Below: George Harrison in 1973, the year that *Living in the Material World* was released. The photo *at right* appeared on the inside jacket cover. Ringo Starr is on the far left, and seated at George Harrison's right is Eric Clapton, who later stole Harrison's wife.

and Jim Morrison of the Doors had overdosed in 1971. The Jefferson Airplane, Quicksilver Messenger Service and Cream were no more. A new crop of personalities and bands had sprung up to take their place, and George Harrison took his place among them. In any case, the quality of the musicianship and the magic of the moment that was present on 29 August 1966 and 1 August 1971 simply was lacking when George Harrison returned to the stage in the mid-1970s.

For Harrison, it was a little like having come down from Olympus to walk among mortal men, and having done so, to become mortal again himself. The dreariness of mortality was further underscored for George when his wife of nearly a decade, Patty Boyd Harrison, left him in favor of his good friend Eric Clapton.

In an era yearning for the excitement of the 'sixties,' George Harrison was not the Beatles. The 'greatest rock and roll band in the world' was now the Rolling Stones, a band which had stood in the shadows of the Beatles from 1964 until 1969. Though well rooted in the 1960s, the Rolling Stones had, in fact, stopped touring in 1966, just as the Beatles had–but they returned to the road in December 1969, after the Beatles' *Abbey Road* album was completed and it had been announced that the Beatles would never go on tour again.

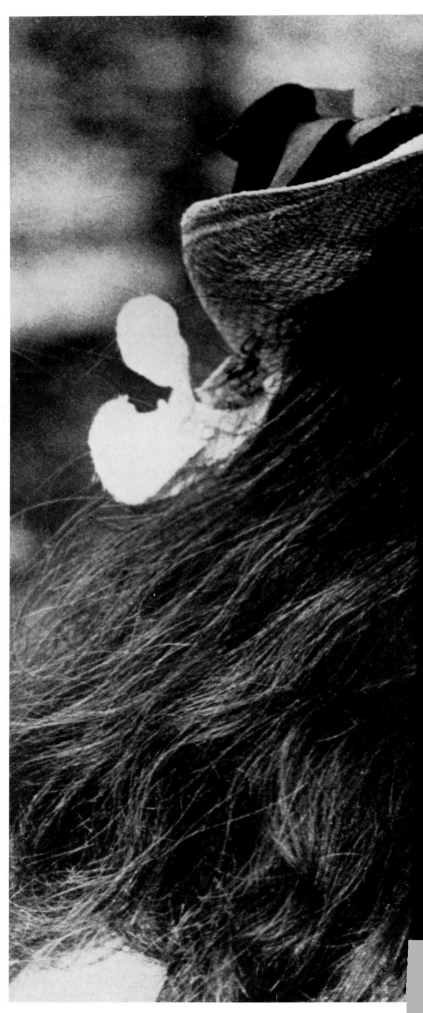

Right: George Harrison in 1974 and on stage *(below)* during his 1975 American tour. Harrison was no longer the superstar he had been during the glory days of the Beatles, and in the early 1970s.

Clearly, Mick Jagger and his entourage were the heirs-apparent to the Beatles' crown. No one *else* could take the Beatles' place. The Stones conducted grand tours of North America in 1969, 1972, 1975 and 1981, with European tours in between. The rock tour was now an art form unto itself, and all its young practitioners, as well the Rolling Stones, had grown up under the musical influence of the band with whom Harrison had toured nine, 10 and 11 years before. It is therefore understandable that, for the entire decade of the 1970s, a band that had stood second only to the Beatles in the 1960s could claim, without question, the title of 'greatest rock and roll band in the world.'

In 1976, George started his own label, called Dark Horse after his 1974 album, and released his *Thirty-Three and a Third* album in November. Capitol and Parlophone responded by releasing the *Best of George Harrison*, a collection of material dating back as far as his early years with the Beatles. George subsequently released three albums on Dark Horse between 1979 and 1982, but retired for five years before coming back with *Cloud Nine* in January 1988.

In the post-Beatles days of the 1970s, Paul McCartney embarked on what was literally a second career. After a solo album in which he played *all* the instruments (*McCartney*, 1970) and another one with just his wife, Linda (*Ram*, 1971), he formed a new group in 1971 and went back on the road. The new group, called Wings, featured Denny Laine (late of the Moody Blues and Electric String Band), Jimmy McCulloch (most recently with Thunderclap Newman) and Denny Seiwell, as well as Paul and Linda McCartney. Howie Casey, a saxophonist, would join the group two years later.

By forming Wings, Paul invited obvious comparisons with the Beatles, but the new collective identity also helped to insulate him from the idea that he was just a 'part' of an entity from the past. Unlike George Harrison, who had toured as himself, Paul was now part of a *new* band, rather than just an ex-member of an *old* band.

Paul went on to record nine albums with Wings over the space of eight years, compared to 13 Parlophone albums over seven years with the Beatles, making his Wings venture a very respect-

Below and right: **Paul McCartney, Linda McCartney and their band Wings during their 1976 concert in San Francisco. Although Paul was the most commercially successful ex-Beatle, many Beatle fans would agree the magic was gone.**

able second career. Wings also toured extensively in the United Kingdom, Europe, the Far East and North America. Their 1976 tour of the latter resulted in the three-disc *Wings Over America* live album.

Nor was Paul particularly adverse to an occasional purely commercial project now and then, such as contributing the title song for the soundtrack of the 1973 James Bond film *Live and Let Die*. The success of Wings, on top of his accumulating residuals from his Beatles career, served to make him the most financially successful ex-Beatle.

In 1982, Paul teamed up with Stevie Wonder for a duet on the song *Ebony and Ivory*, which was released in April both as a single and as part of Paul's solo album, *Tug of War*. Later in the year, Paul recorded *The Girl Is Mine* as a duet with Michael Jackson, which was released on Jackson's album *Thriller* in November. A year later, McCartney and Jackson got together again for *Say Say Say* and *The Man*, which Paul included on his solo album *Pipes of Peace*, released in October, 1983.

In 1984, McCartney completed work on the musical film *Give My Regards to Broad Street*, which opened to mixed reviews and resulted in a soundtrack album featuring new versions of five songs that he had recorded with the Beatles–in addition to a mixture of more recent songs and some all-new material that he had written specifically for the film. *Give My Regards to Broad Street* also featured Ringo Starr as McCartney's drummer, a role

he played on the soundtrack album as well. The *Broad Street* album would be McCartney's last one until his *All the Best*, a two-disc 'greatest hits' retrospective, released in time for Christmas in 1987.

Apple Corps Ltd, the company that had developed so much promising momentum in 1968 (despite its flaws and shortcomings), had become moribund by the middle of 1970. By 1971, Apple *Corps* was nothing more than a very rich *corpse* being fought over by Lee and John Eastman–on behalf of their in-law Paul McCartney–and Allen Klein–on behalf of Paul's former comrades. With only a few exceptions, Apple Records became nothing more than the logo used on albums–by the Beatles, the ex-Beatles and Yoko Ono–which were manufactured and distributed by Parlophone in the United Kingdom and by Capitol in the United States.

In fact, between 1971 and 1975, all Capitol pressings of Beatles records, including pre-1968 releases, carried the familiar green Apple label. The last albums that carried Apple Records labels were the 'greatest hits' albums issued in the autumn, featuring the work of John Lennon (*Shaved Fish*) and Ringo Starr (*Blast from Your Past*), and George Harrison's 1975 single *This Guitar* b/w *Maya Love*.

With the last Beatles album having been released in 1970, Capitol and Parlophone sought to perpetuate the magic by releasing a series of 'greatest hits' albums–not only of the

Left: Paul McCartney with Tracey Ullman in a scene from *Give My Regards to Broad Street*, a musical fantasy. *Above left*: Paul and Linda McCartney on the set of *Give My Regards to Broad Street*. The movie also starred Ringo Starr and his wife Barbara Bach *(above right)*. In the scene *at top*, Paul and his co-stars ham it up for the camera. Note the juxtaposition of the martini and the Foster's Lager in front of the man on the phone. *Overleaf:* In this scene in a converted warehouse, Paul performs one of the movie's 14 songs. Linda McCartney is on the organ, Ringo is on drums and Barbara Bach is in the background.

Paul McCartney's Solo Albums

NOTE: Many of Paul's albums included his wife, Linda East-man McCartney. Her name is cited in those cases in which her role was roughly equal to his. In 1973 Paul formed the band Wings (with Linda as a member), and recorded with them under this name through 1979. All albums were originally released on the Apple/Capitol label in the United States, and on the Apple/Parlophone label in the United Kingdom, unless otherwise specified–with the first five being re-released on Columbia in 1980.

	UK Release Date	US Release Date
McCartney	17 Apr 1970	20 Apr 1970
Ram (With Linda McCartney.)	28 May 1971	17 May 1971
Wild Life (With Wings.)	7 Dec 1971	7 Dec 1971
Red Rose Speedway (With Wings.)	4 May 1973	30 Apr 1973
Band on the Run (With Wings.)	7 Dec 1973	5 Dec 1973
Venus and Mars (With Wings.)	30 May 1975 (Capitol)	27 May 1975 (Capitol)
Wings at the Speed of Sound (With Wings.)	9 Apr 1976 (Capitol)	25 Mar 1976 (Capitol)
Wings over America (Three-disc set recorded live on tour with Wings during 1976.)	10 Dec 1976	10 Dec 1976
London Town (With Wings.)	31 Mar 1978	31 Mar 1978
Wings' Greatest (One-disc Wings 'greatest hits' album.)	1 Dec 1978 (Parlophone)	22 Nov 1978 (Capitol)
Back to the Egg (With Wings.)	8 Jun 1979 (Parlophone)	24 May 1979 (Columbia)
McCartney II	11 Apr 1980 (Parlophone)	
Tug of War (One track with Stevie Wonder.)	26 Apr 1982	27 Apr 1982
Pipes of Peace (Including two duets with Michael Jackson.)	17 Oct 1983 (Parlophone)	26 Oct 1983 (Columbia)
Give My Regards to Broad Street (Soundtrack to the Paul McCartney film of the same name.)	22 Oct 1984 (EMI)	22 Oct 1984 (Columbia)
All The Best (Two-disc 'greatest hits' compilation.)	Dec 1988 (Parlophone)	Dec 1988 (Capitol)

Ringo Starr's Solo Albums

NOTE: All albums were originally released on the Apple/Capitol label in the United States, and on the Apple/Parlophone label in the United Kingdom, unless otherwise noted.

	UK Release Date	US Release Date
Sentimental Journey	27 Mar 1970	28 Sep 1970
Beaucoups of Blues	25 Sep 1970	28 Sep 1970
Ringo (This was the only album of all *new* material recorded after 1969 to include performances by all four Beatles, although none of the tracks feature all four together.)	9 Nov 1973	2 Nov 1973
Goodnight Vienna	15 Nov 1974	18 Nov 1974
Blast from Your Past (A 'greatest hits' album featuring material that Ringo recorded after 1969.)	12 Dec 1975	25 Nov 1975
Ringo's Rotogravure	17 Sep 1976 (Polydor)	27 Sep 1976 (Atlantic)
Ringo the Fourth	20 Sep 1977 (Polydor)	26 Sep 1977 (Atlantic)
Scouse the Mouse (A soundtrack for an animated TV program with half the songs by Ringo.)	9 Dec 1977 (Polydor)	
Bad Boy	21 Apr 1978 (Polydor)	21 Apr 1978 (Portrait)
Stop and Smell the Roses	20 Nov 1981 (RCA)	27 Oct 1981 (Boardwalk)

THE BEATLES' NEXT ALBUM

Since 1970 there have been numerous releases of unauthorized, or 'bootleg,' Beatles albums containing material that was never 'officially' issued by the major record companies. However, the majority of this material is of poor sound quality and/or it has been pressed on inferior vinyl, which enshrouds the music in a haze of surface noise.

Meanwhile, Capitol and EMI (Parlophone) still hold in their vaults immense collections of material of original studio quality that has been heard by few, if any, people since it was recorded in the 1960s. Two Beatles recording sessions, the 1961 studio session with Tony Sheridan and the 1962 live session at the Star Club in Hamburg, Germany, were recorded before the Beatles' contract with EMI, and have

been widely and legally issued and reissued. However, in all the re-releases of the past two decades, no *new* material has been issued by Capitol or Parlophone since 1970, with the exception of the Hollywood Bowl album, released in 1976.

The 1980 Capitol album *The Beatles Rarities* was a disappointment to most fans because it could have given us so much, yet was content to include only slight variations, alternate mixes and versions of songs from out-of-print singles. The last track, a two-second snippet called *Sgt Pepper Inner Groove* was something that had appeared on the Parlophone, but not the Capitol, version of *Sgt Pepper*. The two seconds *were*, however, retained in the 1987 compact disc release in *all* markets. The two seconds, thought by many to contain a 'secret message,' were actually based on an old practice–common thirty years earlier in the era of 78 rpm records–of putting small bits of sound in the inner, or 'runout,' groove of the disks. It is also a little-known fact that these two seconds were preceded by a 15 kilocycle whistle audible *only* to dogs! Rumor has held that it was a 'secret message' to Paul's sheepdog Martha, but records show that its inclusion was John Lennon's idea. The *Rarities* album technically *did* include rarities, but nothing that hadn't been heard before.

Someday–perhaps during the shelf life of this book–Capitol will decide to flick on its flashlight (or EMI its torch), and climb down into their climate-controlled vaults to retrieve some truly significant gems from their own Beatles treasure trove.

The Get Back Sessions

The first stop in a tour of the vaults would probably be the more than one hundred *hours* recorded during January 1969. A dozen songs from these sessions ultimately became the *Let It Be* (1970) album, and alternate versions of two songs had been on the *Get Back* single (1969). Beyond that, a great deal has been 'bootlegged,' but much more remains. This includes the original George Martin version of the *Let It Be* album (*Get Back*)–which was released to radio stations and was quickly recalled in 1969– as well as alternate takes of the same songs, all of which would be interesting to hear, but wouldn't be significantly different from what we already know. The material that *would* be more worthy of release falls into three categories:

(a) Then-current versions of Beatles oldies from *You Really Got a Hold on Me* to *Norwegian Wood*.

(b) Working versions of many of the songs that would later be recorded for *Abbey Road*–versions which tend to be very unlike those which we have come to know.

(c) An immense collection of rock and pop standards from *House of the Rising Sun* to *Michael Row the Boat Ashore* to *Blowin' in the Wind*, and including practically all the memorable hits from the songbooks of Chuck Berry, Little Richard and Elvis Presley.

There is probably enough within the latter category alone to compile a very strong two-disc album.

Alternate Outtakes

This category would tend to include a great many barely distinguishable treatments of familiar songs, but the working versions of *Hey Jude* and *Strawberry Fields Forever* that are known from 'bootlegs' indicate that this could be a source for some outstanding new material. The *Get Back* session probably produced the greatest volume of outtakes, but the remnants of nearly every session at the EMI studios also remain available for release.

Live Recordings

Capitol's 1964 and 1965 efforts to get a live album at the Hollywood Bowl concerts were not the only such occasions in which microphones were dangled off-stage from performing Beatles. For example, the 1964 Carnegie Hall concert was taped, as was the 1965 Shea Stadium concert and the 1966 shows in Tokyo. Indeed, many–if not most–of the Beatles concerts between 1963 and 1966 were recorded either by local promoters, radio stations or the record companies themselves. Only the lack of an agreement on royalties stands in the way of readying this material for release.

Another very important source of live material from this period would be existing studio recordings of broadcasts– from the great many BBC appearances that the Beatles made in 1963 and 1964, to their appearances on the *Ed Sullivan Show*, which began in 1964 and continued (primarily via tape) until nearly the end.

Certainly there is enough material for a very exciting two-disc retrospective of the Beatles' legendary concert career.

All-new Material

Probably the most exciting 'next Beatles album' would be an all-new album. This would include all the Lennon-McCartney and George Harrison songs that were recorded in the various album sessions which were not officially released at any time or in any form. The experience of listening to such an album would be akin to hearing a new Beatles album for the first time–something which many of us haven't experienced in nearly 20 years. It would be–to paraphrase John Lennon from the *Double Fantasy* album–'just like starting over.'

A partial overview of a potential playlist follows below:

1958
1. *In Spite of All the Danger*

1962
2. *Catwalk (aka Catcall)*
3. *Hello Little Girl*
4. *I Lost My Little Girl*
5. *I'll Be on My Way*
6. *Keep Looking This Way*
7. *Looking Glass*
8. *Some Other Guy*
9. *The Years Roll Along*
10. *Thinking of Linking*
11. *Winston's Walk*
12. *Tip of My Tongue*

1963
13. *Bad to Me*
14. *Hold Me Tight*
15. *I'll Keep You Satisfied*
16. *I'm in Love*
17. *Keep Your Hands Off My Baby*
18. *Love of the Loved*

1964
19. *Woman*
20. *Always and Only*
21. *You'll Know What to Do*
22. *From a Window*
23. *I Don't Want to See You Again*
24. *It's for You*
25. *Like Dreamers Do*
26. *Nobody I Know*
27. *One and One Is Two*
28. *A World Without Love*
29. *Nobody I Know*

1965
30. *Auntie Gin's Theme*
31. *Baby Jane*
32. *Eight Arms to Hold You*
33. *If You've Got Troubles*
34. *Maisy Jones*
35. *Rubber Soul*
36. *Scrambled Eggs*
37. *That Means a Lot*
38. *That's a Nice Hat*

1966
39. *Colliding Circles*
40. *Please Don't Bring That Banjo Back*
41. *Pink Litmus Paper Shirt*

1967
42. *Annie*
43. *Anything*
44. *Beatle Talk*
45. *Carnival of Light*
46. *India*
47. *Jessie's Dream*
48. *Not Unknown*
49. *Peace of Mind*
50. *Shirley's Wild Accordion*
51. *Step Inside Love*
52. *What a Shame Mary Jane Had a Pain at the Party*

1968
53. *Happy Birthday Mike Love*
54. *Indian Rope Trick*
55. *Jubilee*
56. *Not Guilty*
57. *Penina*
58. *Revolution 3*
59. *Revolution 4*
60. *Revolution 5*
61. *Revolution 6*
62. *Revolution 7*
63. *Revolution 8*
64. *Revolution*, versions 10 through 22 (?)

1969
65. *All Things Must Pass*
66. *Bad Penny Blues*
67. *Come and Get It*
68. *Four Nights in Moscow*
69. *I Should Like to Live Up a Tree*
70. *Isn't It a Pity*
71. *Just Dancing Around*
72. *Little Eddie*
73. *My Kind of Girl*
74. *Portraits of My Love*
75. *Proud As You Are*
76. *Rocker*
77. *Suicide*
78. *Suzy Parker*
79. *Swinging Days*
80. *Teddy Boy*
81. *What's the News Mary Jane*
82. *When Everybody Comes to Town*
83. *When I Came to Town*
84. *Zero Is Just Another Number*

1970:
85. *Peace of Mind*

INDEX